THE BUMPER BOOK OF JOKES

THE BUMPER BOOK OF JOKES

GYLES BRANDRETH & JANET ROGERS

CHANCELLOR PRESS

1000 Jokes, The Greatest Joke Book Ever Known first published by Carousel 1980
More Crazy Jokes first published by The Hamlyn Publishing Group 1980
Jokes, Jokes, Jokes, A Joke for Every Day of the Year first published by
Corgi-Carousel in 1978

This collected volume first published in 1995 by Chancellor Press
an imprint of Reed International Books Ltd
Michelin House, 81 Fulham Road, London SW3 6RB
and Auckland, Melbourne, Singapore and Toronto

ISBN: 1 85152 826 1

A CIP catalogue record is available for this book from the British Library

Printed and bound in Great Britain by Cox & Wyman Ltd, Reading, Berkshire

THE BUMPER BOOK OF JOKES

1000 JOKES
the greatest joke book ever known

MORE CRAZY JOKES

JOKES, JOKES, JOKES
a joke for every day of the year

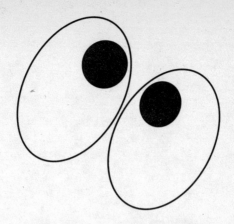

<u>1000 JOKES</u>

the greatest joke book ever known

GYLES BRANDRETH

illustrated by

NICK BERRINGER

Barney: I've owned this car for fifteen years and never had a wreck.
Prospective Buyer: You mean you've owned this wreck for fifteen years and never had a car.

Tony: Father, will you help me find the lowest common denominator in this problem?
Father: Gosh, haven't they found that yet – they were looking for it when I was a lad.

Mr Brown: I haven't seen your dog lately.
Mr Green: No, I had it put down.
Mr Brown: Was it mad?
Mr Green: Well, it wasn't exactly pleased.

What's on telly tonight Jimmy? 'Same as usual – the goldfish bowl and lamp.'

While visiting his friends in County Mayo, Paddy was dismayed when a torrential storm developed. His friend Rory said 'You must stay the night with us – you can't go home in this storm.' 'Thanks very much,' said Paddy, 'I'll just pop home and get me pyjamas.'

Judge: I've decided to give you a suspended sentence.
Prisoner: Thank you, your honour.
Judge: What for? You're going to be hanged.

'Mummy, does God use our bathroom?'
'No darling, why do you ask?'
'Well, every morning Daddy bangs on the door and shouts, 'Oh God, are you still in there?'

Susan: Did Margaret inherit her beauty.
Jean: Yes, her father left her a chemist's shop.

Mother: Why are you keeping this box of earth, Willy?
Willy: It's instant mud-pie mix.

Boy: (Howling) A crab just bit my toe.
Father: Which one?
Boy: How do I know? All crabs look alike to me.

Boss (to department head): How many people work in your office?
Dept. Head: About half of them, sir.

'Why are you scratching yourself, Mary?'
'Nobody else knows where I itch.'

Doctor: Good morning, Mrs Potter, I haven't seen you for a long time.
Mrs P: I know Doctor, I've been ill.

Reggie: We've got a new dog – would you like to come round and play with him?
Ron: Well he sounds very fierce – does he bite?
Reggie: That's what I want to find out.

Waiter: How did you find your chop sir?
Diner: I looked under a chip, and there it was.

Insurance agent: This is a particularly good policy, madam. Under it, we pay up to a thousand pounds for broken arms and legs.
Woman: Good heavens – what do you do with them all?

Mother: Bobby's teacher says he ought to have an encyclopedia.
Father: Let him walk to school like I had to.

Teacher: In what part of the world are people the most ignorant?
Sammy: Tokyo.
Teacher: Why do you say that?
Sammy: Well, my geography book says that's where the population is the densest.

'How long will the next bus be?'
'About eighteen feet.'

Englishman to Paddy: Have you any idea how many sheep there are in this field?
Paddy: Sure – there's three hundred and eighty-six.
Englishman: Good heavens – you're quite right. How did you know?
Paddy: Well, I just counted the legs and divided them by four.

'Doctor, I keep thinking I'm a goat.'
'How long have you had this feeling?'
'Ever since I was a kid.'

Mother: There were two doughnuts in the larder this afternoon, Tommy, now there's only one. How's that?
Tommy: I suppose because it's dark in there – I didn't see the other one.

Safebreaker: I think I need glasses.
Mate: How's that?
Safebreaker: Well, I was twirling the knobs of a safe and an orchestra began to play.

9

Once the night watchman received a pound too much in his pay-packet, but didn't mention it to his boss. But his boss found out and deducted it the following payday.

'Hey,' said the watchman, 'I'm a pound short this week.'

'You didn't say anything last week when you were paid a pound too much, I noticed.'

'No', replied the watchman. 'I can overlook one mistake, but when it happens twice, it's time to speak up!'

A Martian landed at a fun-fair, just as somebody hit the jack-pot and the coins came flooding out. Turning to the machine, the Martian said, 'You shouldn't be out with a cold like that.'

> *Tommy:* Dad, what are four grapes and three grapes?
> *Dad:* Don't you know a simple sum like that – haven't you done a problem like that before?
> *Tommy:* No, dad, we always use bananas at school.

'Doctor – I can't get to sleep at night.'
'Don't worry – lie on the edge of the bed and you'll soon drop off.'

Teacher: Jimmy, give me a sentence with the word 'centimetre' in it.
Jimmy: Er … My sister was coming home by bus and I was centimetre.

Mother: Bobby, have you given the goldfish fresh water today?
Bobby: No, they haven't finished what I gave them yesterday.

Dad: How were your exam questions Ben?
Ben: Fine – but I had difficulty with the answers.

'That's a dreadful bump on your head, Patrick, how did it happen?'
'Somebody threw tomatoes at me.'
'Heavens, how could tomatoes cause a bump like that?
'They were in a tin.'

Frankie: Which month has twenty-eight days?
Peggy: All of them.

Mike: I saw all your chickens out in your front garden yesterday.
Patrick: Yes, they heard that men were coming to lay a pavement, and they wanted to see how it was done.

Teacher: Why do we sometimes call the Middle Ages the Dark Ages?
Betty: Because they had so many knights.

A little boy saw a grass snake for the first time.
'Mother,' he cried, 'here's a tail without a body.'

Teacher: Polly, how can you prove the world is round?
Polly: I never said it was, miss.

A boy and an old man were standing in the aisle of a crowded bus. 'Pass farther down the bus,' called the conductor.
'He's not my father,' said the boy, 'he's my grandfather.'

In St James's Park a man holding a
penguin went up to a policeman.
'I've found this penguin,' he said.
'What shall I do with him?'

'You'd better take him to the zoo,'
said the policeman. The next day,
the policeman again saw the same
man with the penguin. 'I thought I
told you to take him to the zoo,' he
said.

'I did that yesterday,' said the
man. 'And today I'm taking him to
the pictures.'

Captain: Why didn't you stop the
ball?
Goalie: I thought that's what the
nets were for.

Pupil (indignantly): I don't think I
deserve a nought on this test.
Teacher: Neither do I, but it's the
lowest mark I can give you.

Joe: I fell over twenty feet last night.
Max: Good heavens – weren't you hurt?
Joe: No – I was just trying to get to my seat in the cinema.

Two flies were on Robinson Crusoe's head.
'Goodbye for now,' said one. 'I'll see you on Friday.'

Sign in a police station:
'Thirty days hath September, April, June and the Speed Offender.'

Big man (in a theatre, to a small boy sitting behind him) Can you see, sonny?
Boy: No, sir, not at all.
Big man: Then just watch me and laugh when I do.

Vicar: Now, Georgie, you shouldn't fight, you should learn to give and take.
Georgie: I did, I gave him a black eye and I took his apple.

'My uncle has 500 men under him.'
'He must be very important.'
'Not really – he's a maintenance man in a cemetery.'

14

Richard: Would you punish a boy for something he didn't do?
Teacher: Of course not.
Richard: That's good. I haven't done my homework.

The new workman opened his lunch-packet and took out two sandwiches. He opened one and his face fell. 'Fish-paste,' he said. He looked again, and the same thing happened, 'More fish-paste,' he grumbled. When he was disappointed for the third time, his mate said, 'Why don't you get your wife to make you something else.' 'I'm not married,' said the man, 'I make these sandwiches myself.'

'Waiter, there's a dead fly in my soup'
'Yes, sir, I know – it's the heat that kills them.'

The aeroplane was so old, it even had an outside lavatory.

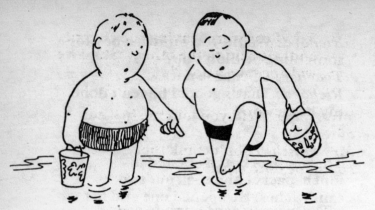

Two boys were paddling in the sea at Brighton.
'Gosh, ain't your feet dirty,' said one.
'Yes,' replied the other, 'we didn't come last year.'

Little Bernie was taking his new dog for a walk when a policeman stopped him.
'Has your dog got a licence?' the policeman asked.
'Oh no.' answered Bernie. 'He's not old enough to drive.'

Teacher: Sidney, can you tell me how fast light travels?
Sidney: I don't know, but it always gets here too early in the morning.

Teacher: Why were you absent yesterday, Tommy?
Tommy: The doctor said I had acid indigestion.
Teacher: Then you'd better stop drinking acid.

Two fleas were leaving the cinema, and one said to the other: 'Shall we walk or take a dog?'

Mrs Jones: Will you join me in a cup of tea?
Mrs Smith: I don't think there'd be room for both of us.

The visitor from London was boasting in a Manchester pub about all the famous people who had been born in London. 'Have many big men been born in Manchester?' he asked the landlord. 'None', said the landlord, 'only babies.'

Betty: That man next door has got carrots growing out of his ears.
Harold: How terrible!
Betty: It certainly is. He planted parsnips.

'Did you know that deep breathing kills germs?'
'Yes, but how do you get them to breathe deeply?'

Do you know the one about the cornflakes and the rice krispies who had a fight?
– I can only tell you a little at a time as it's a serial.

What is red and stupid?
A blood-clot.

Big brother (to shop assistant): My
mother would like a dozen nappies
for the new baby.
Assistant: Here we are. That will be
three pounds for the nappies, and
75 pence for the tax.
Big brother: Don't bother about the
tacks. My mother uses safety pins.

Did you hear about the vegetarian
cannibal?
– He would only eat Swedes.

Nurse: Well, Mr Smith, you seem to
be coughing much more easily this
morning.
Mr Smith: That's because I've been
practising all night.

Traffic policeman: When I saw you
driving down the high-street, lady, I
said to myself, 'Sixty at least.'
Lady Driver: Oh no, officer – it's just
this hat makes me look older.

Should you stir your tea with your
left hand or your right hand?
Neither – you should use your spoon.

Dentist: Please stop howling. I haven't even touched your tooth yet.
Patient: I know, but you're treading on my foot.

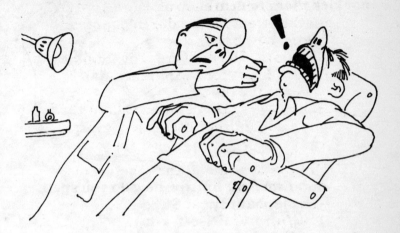

Teacher: Can you name four animals of the cat family?
Mary: Mother cat, father cat, and two kittens.

Advertisement in local paper:
LOST – WRIST WATCH BY A LADY WITH A CRACKED FACE.

Nobby: Dad, I'm too tired to do my homework.
Dad: Now, my lad, hard work never killed anyone yet.
Nobby: Well, I don't want to run the risk of being the first.

Customer: I'd like some poison for mice please.
Chemist: Have you tried Boots?
Customer: I want to poison them, not kick them to death.

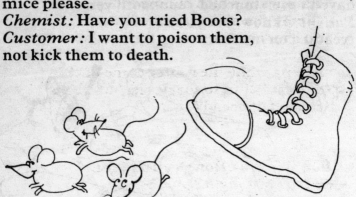

Teacher: Jimmy, how do you spell elephant?
Jimmy: E-l-e-f-a-n-t.
Teacher: The dictionary spells it 'e-l-e-p-h-a-n-t'.
Jimmy: You didn't ask me how the dictionary spelt it.

Passenger: Is this my train?
Inspector: No, it belongs to British Rail?
Passenger: Don't be funny – I mean can I take this train to London?
Inspector: No, sir, it's much too heavy.

Monty: Is it really bad luck to have a black cat follow you?
Mike: Well, it depends on whether you're a man or a mouse.

An American visiting London saw a restaurant which claimed they could supply any dish requested.
So he asked the waiter for kangaroo on toast.
After a while the waiter came back and said, 'I'm so sorry, sir, but we've run out of bread.'

Don: Why did Ron sleep under the oil tank last night?
John: Because he wanted to get up oily this morning.

Sammy: Mummy, how much am I worth to you?
Mother: Why, you're worth more than a million to me, dear.
Sammy: Well, could you advance me twenty-five pence?

Teacher: Brown, stop showing off. Do you think you're the teacher of this class?
Brown: No sir.
Teacher: Right, then stop behaving like a fool.

Customer: Waiter, I've only got one piece of meat.
Waiter: Just a moment, sir, and I'll cut it in two.

Customer: I'd like to try that dress in the window.
Assistant: I'm sorry, madam, I'm afraid you'll have to use the fitting room, like everybody else.

There was an Arab who was so fat, his camel had its hump underneath.

How do you keep flies out of the kitchen?
– Put all the rubbish in the lounge.

Customer to Bank Manager: How do I stand for a £3,000 loan?
B. Manager: You don't – you grovel.

Would you like to buy a pocket calculator, sir?'
'No thanks, I know how many pockets I've got.'

Customer in butcher's shop: Have you got a sheep's head?
Butcher: No, it's just the way I part my hair.

Hotel receptionist in France, to Englishman: Are you a foreigner?
Englishman: Certainly not. I'm British!

Mother Lion: Son, what are you doing?
Baby Lion: I'm chasing a man round a tree.
Mother Lion: How often must I tell you not to play with your food.

Father: Freddie, you're a pig. Do you know what a pig is?
Freddie: Sure, dad. A pig is a hog's little boy.

Nurse: Can I take your pulse?
Patient: Why? Haven't you got one of your own?

What did the gas-meter say to the tenpence piece?
- Glad you dropped in, I was just going out.

Barber: Were you wearing a red scarf when you came in?
Customer: No.
Barber: Oh, then I must have cut your throat.

A man came back to the car dealer from whom he had bought a new car. 'I believe you gave me a guarantee with my car,' he said.
'That's right, sir,' the dealer answered. 'We will replace anything that breaks.'
'Fine. I need a new garage door.'

Visitor: Is this a healthy place to live?
Local yokel: Yessir. When I arrived here I couldn't walk or eat solid food.
Visitor: What was the matter with you?
Local yokel: Nothing – I was born here.

Doctor: Mrs Smith, you have acute angina.
Patient: I came to be examined, not admired.

Estate agent to young couple: First you tell me what you can afford, then we'll have a good laugh about it, and go on from there.

Angry boss to office boy: You are late again this morning.
Office boy: I overslept.
Angry boss: You mean you sleep at home *as well?*

'Will the band play anything I request?'
'Certainly, sir.'
'Well, ask them to play chess.'

Harry: This lamb is very tough.
Polly: I'm sorry – the butcher said it was a spring lamb.
Harry: Well, I must be eating one of the springs.

Proud Mother: My baby is a year old now, and he's been walking since he was eight months old.
Bored visitor: Really? He must be awfully tired.

Rich customer on phone to fishmonger: Please send me a dozen oysters, not too large, not too small, not very old, not tough and not sandy.
Fishmonger: Yes, madam. With pearls or without?

Judge: Have you been up before me before?
Prisoner: I don't know, what time do you get up?

Father was showing Tommy the family album, and came across a picture of himself and his wife on their wedding day.
'Was that the day Mummy came to work for us?' Tommy asked.

Disgusted diner: What do you call this stuff, coffee or tea?
Waiter: What do you mean, sir?
Diner: It tastes like paraffin.
Waiter: Well, if it tastes like paraffin, it must be coffee; our tea tastes like turpentine.

1st Soldier: Our C.O. rose from the ranks.
2nd Soldier: Is that so?
1st Soldier Yes – he used to be a taxi-driver.

Wife: Do you have a good memory for faces?
Husband: Yes – why?
Wife: I've just broken your shaving mirror.

Motorist: When I bought this car you said it was rust free. The underneath's covered with it.
Dealer: Yes, sir. The car's rust free. We didn't charge for it.

Have you heard the one about the man who always wore sunglasses?
– He took a dim view of things.

'I wonder why these seaside boarding house keepers are called land-ladies?'
'Because they charge the earth'

Cinema attendant: That's the sixth ticket you've bought.
Customer: I know – there's a girl in there that keeps tearing them up.

Susie: Mother, what was the name of the last station our train stopped at?
Mother: I don't know – can't you see I'm reading?
Susie: Well, it's too bad, because little Benny got off there.

Teacher: Bobby, can you name the four seasons?
Bobby: Salt, pepper, vinegar and mustard.

Sergeant (to new recruit): And what were you then, before you joined the army?
New Recruit: Happy, sergeant.

28

Doctor: I am sorry to have to tell you that you may have rabies, and it could prove fatal.
Patient: Well, doctor, please give me pencil and paper.
Doctor: To make your Will?
Patient: No – I want to make a list of people I want to bite.

Teacher: If you found five pence in one pocket and ten pence in the other, what would you have?
Willy: Somebody else's trousers.

Peter: My teacher was cross because I didn't know where the pyramids were.
Mother: (absently) Well, dear, next time remember where you put things.

Betty: What do you think of Red China?
Mary: Well, it would look nice with a white tablecloth.

Jack: What did the bald man say when he received a comb for his birthday?
Tom: I don't know, what did he say?
Jack: Thanks very much, I'll never part with it.

Sally: Did you see the guards change when you were in London?
Lulu: No, they always pulled the blinds down.

The cannibal came home to find his wife chopping up snakes and a very small man. 'Oh no,' he groaned. 'Not snake and pygmy pie again!'

'Why are you jumping up and down?'
'I've just taken some medicine and I forgot to shake the bottle.'

Writer: I took up writing full-time a year ago.
Friend: Have you sold anything?
Writer: Yes – my t.v., all the furniture, the house ...

It's easy to make time fly. Just throw an alarm clock over your shoulder.

'My husband is so ugly when he goes
to the zoo he has to buy two tickets:
one to get in and one to get out.'

Army colonel: I'd like some pepper,
my good man.
Shop assistant: Certainly, sir. What
sort would you like – white pepper or
black pepper?'
Army colonel: Neither – I want
writing pepper.

Teacher: Which is farther away –
Canada or the moon?
Bobby: Canada.
Teacher: Why do you say that?
Bobby: We can see the moon, and we
can't see Canada.

Customer: You said this simple
gadget was foolproof. I can't see how
to use it.
Shopkeeper: Then it's what it says it
is. It proves you're a fool.

A guide was showing a man from Texas Niagara Falls.
Guide: I'll bet you don't have anything like this in Texas.
Texan: Nope, but we got plumbers who can fix it.

How can you decide whether to use a screw or a nail when doing carpentry? Drive in a nail – if the wood splits, you should have used a screw.

Sign in a Volkswagen factory: THINK BIG – and you're fired.

A man was driving down a one-way street the wrong way and was stopped by a policeman. 'This is a one-way street,' said the officer. 'I know,' said the motorist, 'I'm only going one way.'

Greengrocer: Yes, madam, they're beautiful tomatoes – they come from the Canaries.
Customer: Fancy, I always thought they were grown, not laid.

'I've never been troubled with back-seat drivers.'
'Why, what car do you drive?'
'A hearse.'

A woman dashed into a hardware shops and asked to be served at once. 'Give me a mouse-trap please.' she gasped. 'I've got to catch a train.' 'I'm sorry,' said the assistant. 'We haven't got any as big as that.'

Teacher: What is the difference between the death rate in Victorian England and the present day?
Pupil: It's the same, miss. One per person.

'Do you write with your left hand or your right hand?'
– Neither – I write with a ball-point pen.

'My brother bought a baby car – but it won't go anywhere without a rattle.'

Customer: Those strawberries look as if they were picked weeks ago, yet your notice says Fresh Today.
Greengrocer: That's right. This notice *is* fresh today. I've just written it out.

Mr Johnson: Are you using your mower this afternoon?
Mr Smith: Yes.
Mr Johnson: Fine. Then can I borrow your tennis racket, as you won't be needing it.

Salesman: Little boy, is your mother at home?
Willy: Yes, sir.
Salesman (after knocking for some time and getting no reply): I thought you said she was at home.
Willy: She is, but we don't live here.

Judge: Tell me, why did you park
your car here?
Motorist: Well there was a sign
which said FINE FOR PARKING.

'I've just lost my dog.'
'Well, why don't you put an
advertisement in the paper?'
'What's the good of that – my dog
can't read.'

Mother: Freddie, why is your face so
red?
Freddie: I was running up the street
to stop a fight.
Mother: That's a very nice thing to
do. Who was fighting?
Freddie: Me and Jackie Smith.

Dolphins are so intelligent that
within a few weeks of captivity they
can train a man to stand on the edge
of their pool and throw them fish
three times a day.

Mother: Did you behave well in
church today, Marjie?
Marjie: I certainly did. A nice man
offered me a plate full of money, and
I said, 'No thank you."

35

Pamela: I've added these figures ten times, miss.
Teacher: Good girl.
Pamela: And here are the ten answers.

'I went to the dentist this morning.'
'Does your tooth still hurt?'
'I don't know – the dentist kept it.'

A beautiful young lady kissed a Prince last night – and he turned into a toad.

Bill: Do you have holes in your trousers?
Jim: Certainly not.
Bill: Then how do you get your legs through?

Sol: I say, that's a hundred-pound cheque you're writing.
Gus: Yes, I'm sending it to my sister for her birthday.
Sol: But you haven't signed it.
Gus: No, I don't want her to know who sent it.

Due to a strike at the meteorological office, there will be no weather tomorrow.

A grammar school boy took out of the library a book whose cover read How to Hug, but discovered to his disappointment that it was Volume 7 of the Encyclopedia.

A man walked into a baker's shop and asked for a bath bun.
'Certainly, sir,' replied the assistant. 'Anything else?'
'Yes,' said the man, 'I'll have a sponge to go with it.'

Percy: How do fishermen make their nets, Dad?
Dad: Easily. They just take a lot of holes and sew them together.

Customer: Ironmonger, have you got one inch nails?
Ironmonger: Yes, sir.
Customer: Then will you scratch my back please – it's itching something awful.

Two Red Indians were watching some distant smoke-signals. When they were finished, one Indian turned to the other and said, 'We shall have to do something about Little Big Horse, his spelling is something awful.'

Do you know how to make a slow horse fast?
No – do you?
Yes – just don't give him anything to eat.

Last week a man fell into a keg of beer and came to a bitter end.

Dentist: I'm afraid your teeth will have to come out.
Patient: Oh dear, that will be an awful wrench.

'My dog has no nose.'
'How does it smell?'
'Terrible.'

Wholesome – the only thing from
which you can take the whole and
still have some left.

'Every day my dog and I go for a
tramp in the woods.'
'Does the dog enjoy it?'
'O yes – but the tramp is a bit fed up.'

'I hear you've fallen in love with
Dracula.'
'Yes, it was love at first bite.'

Doorman: Your car is at the door,
sir.
Car owner: Yes, I can hear it
knocking.

Young man: Er, excuse me – but
would you come out with me tonight.
Dolly: Oh, I don't go out with perfect
strangers.
Young man: Who said I was perfect?

Barry: Howmany balls of string would it take to reach the moon?
Garry: Only one – if it were long enough.

Mother: Now, Monty, you know you're not supposed to eat with your knife.
Monty: I know, ma, but my fork leaks.

A drunk raced after a fire engine, but collapsed exhausted after a hundred yards, 'Alright,' he shouted, 'keep your rotten ice-cream.'

One egg boiling in a pan said to
another egg in the pan: 'Gosh, it's
hot in here.'
Said the other egg: 'Wait till you get
out, you'll have your head bashed in.'

Patient: Will my measles be better
next week, doctor?
Doctor: I don't like to make rash
promises.

Customer (to Bank Manager): Will
you help me out, please?
B.M. Certainly – go through that
door there.

Old man (to his wife): What on earth
are you doing?
Wife: Knitting up some barbed-wire
fence.
Old man: How can you do that?
Wife: I'm using steel wool.

1st Ghost: I see 'Psycho' is on telly
again tonight.
2nd Ghost: Yes – last time I saw it, it
nearly frightened the life into me.

After the dance, the young man asked the young lady if he could see her home – so she showed him a photograph of it.

Bert: Mum, there's a man with a bill at the door.
Mummy: Don't be silly, dear, it must be a duck with a hat on.

Bright Billy: Dad, is your watch going?
Dad: Yes, of course it is.
B. Billy: Then when's it coming back?

Pedestrian – a person who can be easily reached by car.

'Will you kiss me?'
'But I have scruples.'
'That's alright – I've been vaccinated.'

Man on telephone to Weather Bureau: What are the chances of a shower today?
Weatherman: It's okay with me, sir. If you want one, take one.

Patient: And when my right arm is better, doctor, will I be able to play the trumpet?
Doctor: Of course you will.
Patient: How marvellous – I never could before.

Winnie: I must say Norman is very full of himself, isn't he?
Babs: Yes – especially when he bites his nails.

Lady on phone: Doctor, what can I do – my little boy has swallowed my pen?
Doctor: Use a pencil.

Teacher: Now, Jackie, what is the highest form of animal life?
Jackie: I think it's the giraffe, miss.

'Why were you driving so fast?' said the policeman to the speeding motorist.
'Well, my brakes are faulty and I wanted to get home before I had an accident.'

43

The absent-minded professor was going round and round in a swing door. 'What's the matter?' asked a friend.
'I can't remember whether I'm on my way in or on my way out,' replied the Prof.

Harry: Have you read the Bible?
Sally: No, I'm waiting for the film.

Friend: Your dog's got a funny bark.
Dog-owner: Yes, he's a dachshund, and speaks with a German accent.

Teacher: Now, Brian, what is the formula for water?
Brian: H,I,J,K,L,M,N,O.
Teacher: Now then, you're not in the nursery you know.
Brian: Well, you did say it was H to O.

The cantankerous old lady who lived alone had not been invited to her neighbour's picnic. On realizing their oversight the neighbours sent round to ask her to come along.
'It's too late now,' she snapped. 'I've already prayed for rain.'

Patient: What can you give me for flat feet, Doctor?
Doctor: Have you tried a bicycle-pump?

He: Why were the Red Indians the first people in North America?
She: Because they had reservations.

Teacher: In some countries they use fish as a means of exchange.
Willy: Gee, it must be messy getting chocolate out of a machine.

What did the hamburger say to the tomato?
– That's enough of your sauce.

Guide (on safari): Quick, sir, shoot that leopard right on the spot.
Lord Clarence: Be specific, man, which spot?

The more we study, the more we know.
The more we know, the more we forget.
The more we forget, the less we know.
So, why study?

Notice in a pet shop: IN THE INTEREST OF DOGS, HYGIENE IS NOT PERMITTED IN THIS SHOP.

Woodwork master: What are you making there, Jimmy?
Jimmy: A portable, sir.
W. master: A portable what?
Jimmy: I don't know yet, sir. I've only made the handle.

The life-long Socialist dying on his bed, decided to become a Tory. When asked why he was doing this, he told his puzzled family: 'I'd rather it was a Tory that died than a Socialist.'

The fat lady walked into the dress shop. 'I'd like to see a dress that would fit me.' she told the assistant. 'So would I,' said the tactless assistant.

Teacher: What family does the rhinoceros belong to?
David: I don't know, miss, nobody in our street has one.

'Waiter, have you got frogs' legs?'
'No, sir, I always walk this way.'

A woman took her dog back to the pet shop and complained 'This dog makes a shocking mess all over the house, and you told me he was house-trained.'
'That's right, he is,' said the shop owner. 'He won't go anywhere else!'

Lady: Waiter, please bring me coffee without cream.
Waiter: I'm afraid we've run out of cream. Would you like it without milk instead?

Penicillin – the present for the man who has everything.

Visitor: Does your dog like children?
Dog-owner: Yes, but he prefers biscuits and gravy.

Waiter: What can I get you sir?
Diner: Steak and chips.
Waiter: Would you like anything with it sir?
Diner: If it's anything like the last I ate here, you'd better bring me a hammer and chisel.

One day a worried-looking man knocked at a lady's door. 'I'm very sorry, lady,' he said, 'I've just run over your cat and I'd like to replace it.'
'Well,' said the lady doubtfully, 'can you catch mice?'

48

The Scotsman was asked for a donation to the orphanage, so he sent them two orphans.

Willy came home from Sunday School and asked his mother:
'Do people really come from dust'.
'In a way', said his mother.
'And do they go back to dust?
'Yes, in a way.'
'Well, mother, I've just looked under my bed, and there's somebody either coming or going.'

Customer: Why is this chop so very tough?
Waiter: Well, sir, it's a karate chop.

Patient: I still feel very tired, doctor.
Doctor: Didn't you take those sleeping pills I gave you?
Patient: Well, they looked so peaceful in the little bottle that I didn't like to wake them up.

A farmer had a large hay field. His son didn't want to stay on the farm so he moved to town, but the only job he could get was shining shoes, so now the farmer makes hay while the son shines.

What were Tarzan's last words?
– Who greased the vine?

Teacher: How many feet are there in
a yard?
Joe: It depends how many people
are standing in it.

Cecil: Do you know how many days
belong to the year?
Claud: All of them, I suppose.
Cecil: Nope, just 325. The rest are
Lent.

1st Cannibal: I feel sick every time I
eat a missionary.
2nd Cannibal: That's because you
can't keep a good man down.

How do you get down from a camel?
– You don't. You get down from a
duck.

'My mother gave Dad some
soapflakes instead of cornflakes for
his breakfast, by mistake.'
'Was he cross?'
'He certainly was. He foamed at the
mouth.'

'My husband is very religious – he
won't work if there's a Sunday in the
week.'

A boy took his dog with him to the
cinema to see 'Gone With The Wind'.
The usherette was about to make the
dog leave when she saw it seemed to
be enjoying the film, so she let it stay.
After it was over, she spoke to the
boy. 'I was surprised to see your dog
enjoying the film,' she said.
'So was I,' said the boy. 'He didn't
like the book one bit.'

Have you heard the one about
quicksand? It takes a long time to
sink in.

Customer (to Barber): That's a lot
to pay for a haircut – after all I'm
nearly bald.
Barber: Yes, that's the trouble. It
was the time taken to find it to cut
which cost the money.

Footballer: I've a good idea to improve the team.
Manager: Good. When are you leaving?

Sid: My father can play the piano by ear.
Don: That's nothing – my father fiddles with his whiskers.

Father: Don't go into the water right after lunch.
It's dangerous to swim on a full stomach.
Son: That's alright, I'll swim on my back.

Bus conductor: This coin you've just given me has a hole in it.
Young passenger: So has this ticket you've just given me.

'I was an unwanted child – my mother wanted puppies.'

Mr Pigeon to Mrs Pigeon: Look, dear, there's a railway station – let's fly over it and do some train-spotting.

The old lady was being interviewed by the local press after she had reached the age of 110. 'What do you think is the reason for your long life?' they asked her.
She thought for a while. 'Well,' she said, 'I suppose it's because I was born such a long time ago.

Tim: Mother, you'd better come out. I've just knocked over the ladder at the side of the house.
Mother: I'm busy – run and tell your father.
Tim: He already knows. He's hanging from the roof.

Mr Brown: I've noticed Mr Johnson's manners have improved lately.
Mrs Brown: Yes, he got a job in a refinery.

My wife reads the obituary columns every morning, and can't understand how people keep dying in alphabetical order.

Barber (to boy customer): Who cut your hair last time – your Mum?
Boy: Yes, she did it with a pudding basin.
Barber: I thought so. Next time, tell her to use scissors.

Blenkinsop: One of my ancestors died at Waterloo.
Bloggs: Really, which platform?

Two children were watching a motor-boat pulling a man on skis across a lake. 'What makes that boat go so fast?' asked little Lucy.
'It's because that man on the string is chasing it,' said her brother.

Mother: Didn't I tell you to let me know when the soup began to boil?
Joe: Yes, and I'm telling you. It was half past one.

Did you hear about the ex-
policeman who became a barber?
He kept nicking his customers.

Teacher: When do the leaves begin
to turn?
Student: The night before an
examination.

Gormless Gus went into a shop with
a mince pie stuck in each ear.
'Excuse me,' said the shop assistant,
'but you've got mince pies in your
ears.'
'You'll have to speak up,' said
Gormless Gus. 'I've got mince
pies in my ears.'

'Come in number 9 – your time is
up.'
'But we've only got eight boats.'
'Are you in trouble Number 6?'

55

Postman: I have a parcel here but the name on it is obliterated.
Jackson: Can't be for me then, my name's Jackson.

The poet had been droning on at the party about his various sources of inspiration. 'Yes,' he told the young girl, 'I'm at present collecting some of my better poems to be published posthumously.'
'Lovely,' said the girl. 'I shall look forward to it.'

Which pantomime is about a cat in a chemist's shop?
– Puss in Boots.

Harry and Larry were given a toboggan for Christmas. After they had been out playing in the snow Larry was in tears.
'Now, Harry,' said father, 'I told you to let Larry use the toboggan half the time.'
'So I did,' said Harry, 'I had it going down, and he had it going up.'

Why do cows in Switzerland have bells round their necks?
– Because their horns don't work.

In Dodge City the Sheriff arrested
Lulu Belle for wearing a taffeta
dress.
'What's the charge, sheriff?' she
asked.
'Rustlin' of course,' he replied.

Dan: When I grow up I'm going to be
a policeman and follow my father's
footsteps.
Stan: I didn't know your father was a
policeman.
Dan: He's not, he's a burglar.

Tommy: Are worms good to eat?
Dad: I shouldn't think so. Why?
Tommy: There was one in your pie.

'Could you see me across the road,
constable?'
'I could see you a mile away,
madam.'

Mother: How was the choir's Christmas visit to the Old Folk's Home?

Olive: Oh, we gave them a couple of Carols.

Mother: 'Away in a Manger?'

Olive: No, Carol Jones and Carol Taylor.

Teacher: What is pop-art?

Freddie: It's what Dad says to Mum when he's just going to pop-art for a quick one.

Diner: Where's the rum in this rum-pie?

Waiter: Well, would you expect to find a dog in a dog biscuit?

'Is your new horse well-behaved?'
'Oh yes. When we come to a fence, he stops and lets me go over first.'

Husband: What would you like for your birthday?

Wife: Oh ... let it be a surprise.

Husband: Right .. BOO!

Jill: Daddy, Jack's broken my new doll.

Daddy: How did he do that?

Jill: I hit him on the head with it.

Lady, visiting artist in his studio; Do you like painting people in the nude?
Artist: No, personally I prefer painting with my clothes on.

Mother: Willy, it's rude to keep stretching across the table for the cake. Haven't you got a tongue?
Willy: Yes, but my arm's longer.

A woman was driving the wrong way down a one-way street and was stopped by a policeman.
'Didn't you see the arrows?' he asked.
'Arrows? I didn't even see the Indians.'

Little Caroline was drawing a Nativity picture – there was Mary and Joseph, shepherds and wise men.
'What's that in the corner?' asked her teacher.
'That's their telly, of course,' replied Caroline.

Percy: I've just got a bottle of vodka for my mother-in-law.
Bertie: Sounds like a good swap.

Teacher: Now, Brenda, how many fingers have you?
Brenda: Ten.
Teacher: Right. Now if you lost four of them in an accident, what would you have?
Brenda: No more piano lessons.

Old Lady (to Baker): What's that loaf up there?
Assistant: That's a tin loaf, madam.
Old Lady: Oh I think I'd better have something a bit softer. My teeth aren't what they used to be.

Charlie had eaten too many jam tarts, and clutched his stomach and groaned.
'Are you in pain?' asked his mother.
'No,' moaned Charlie, 'the pain's in me.'

Friend: And what are you going to give your baby brother for his birthday, Janet?
Janet: I don't know – last year I gave him measles.

Cousin Ted: How's your father getting on with his new dairy farm?
Cousin Ned: He makes all the cows sleep on their backs, so the cream will be on top in the morning.

Shop owner: Yes, madam, these are the same pork pies we've had for years.
·*Customer:* Could you show me some you've had more recently please?

Our family was so poor, my sister was made in Hong Kong.

Anybody who boasts about his ancestors is admitting that his family is better dead than alive.

Mr Mouse discovered Mrs Mouse drowning in a bowl of water, so he dragged her out and gave her mouse to mouse resuscitation.

Lucy was finishing her prayers. 'God bless my mother and my father and make Rotterdam the capital of Holland.'
'Why, Lucy' asked her mother. 'Why did you say that?'
'Because,' explained Lucy, 'that's what I wrote on my exam-paper.'

Rose found her sister Mary wearing her fur-lined rubber shoes, and demanded to know the reason why.
'Well,' said Mary, 'you wouldn't like me to get your new silver dancing pumps wet, would you?'

Our neighbour believes in free speech. Particularly long distance phone calls from our house.

The visitor stared in amazement at the child knocking nails into the posh Scandinavian furniture.
He turned to his host. 'Don't you find it expensive to let your son play games like that?' he asked.
'Not really,' replied the host. 'I get the nails wholesale.'

Policeman: I'm sorry sonny, but you need a permit to fish here.
Sonny: That's alright, thanks. I'm doing okay with a worm.

Young Tim was raking leaves with his father who was telling him about how the fairies turned the leaves brown. He looked up pityingly at his father. 'Haven't you ever heard of photosynthesis?' he asked him.

Dora: Listen, I can hear the band playing The Men of Harlech?
Mona: Really – who's winning?

Music Teacher: What is the meaning of 'allegro'?
Susie: It's what a line of chorus girls make with their legs.

Gordon: How's your sister getting on with her reducing diet?
Charlie: Fine – she disappeared last week.

Morris: Can you spell blind pig?
Norman: B-l-i-n-d p-i-g.
Morris: No. It's b-l-n-d p-g. With two i's he wouldn't be blind.

Ramon from Madrid was on holiday
in Killarney and talking to Patrick.
'We have a word in Spanish,' he said,
Mañana. It means tomorrow –
always tomorrow.
Do you have a word for it in your
country?'
After a pause Patrick said, 'No, I
don't think we have any word with
such a sense of urgency.'

> *Brown:* I cured my son of biting his
> nails.
> *Green:* Oh, how did you manage
> that?
> *Brown:* I knocked all his teeth out.

What does 36 inches make in
Glasgow?
–One Scotland yard.

> The lazy man tried to get a job at the
> Bakers because he thought life
> would be one long loaf.

> *Motorist:* Can you tell me the way to
> Bath?
> *Policeman:* I always use soap and
> water myself.

'Susan I think your husband dresses
nattily!'
'Natalie who?'

Visiting the Modern Art Museum, a lady turned to an attendant standing nearby. 'This,' she said, 'I suppose is one of those hideous representations you call modern art?'

'No, madam,' replied the attendant. 'That one's called a mirror.'

The Irishman wanted to go surf-riding, but he couldn't persuade the horse to go into the water.

English Teacher: Simon, I'd like you to make up a sentence with a direct object.
Simon: (after a pause): 'Miss, everybody thinks you are beautiful and clever.'
English Teacher: Well thank you, but what is the direct object?
Simon: A good report, Miss.

Eve: That's a nice coat you're wearing – what fur is it?
Amy: I don't know, but everytime I pass a dog, the fur goes up at the back.

'I say, what a lovely colour that cow over there is.'
'It's a jersey.'
'Oh – I thought it was her skin.'

A very fat lady sitting on the bus, noticed three elderly ladies standing. Turning to the man next to her, she said: 'If you were a gentleman you'd get up and let one of those ladies sit down.'
'If you were a lady,' he replied, 'you get up and let all three of them sit down.'

'The only thing my husband ever achieved on his own is his moustache.'

Mother: Why is your little brother crying?
Billy: Because I won't give him my piece of cake.
Mother: Is his piece gone?
Billy: Yes – he cried when I ate that, too.

Sign in a Police Station: IT TAKES ABOUT 3500 BOLTS TO PUT A MOTOR CAR TOGETHER BUT ONLY ONE NUT TO SCATTER IT ALL OVER THE ROAD.

Molly: Why does your brother spend so much time playing football?
Polly: Oh, he just does it for kicks.

New Husband: Just think darling – we've now been married for twenty-four hours!
New Wife: Yes, darling, and it seems like only yesterday.

'My wife and I don't argue – she goes her way, and I go hers.'

A chap was spreading powder in the middle of the road. 'What do you think you're doing?' asked a policeman.
'Spreading crocodile powder,' said the man.
'There's no crocodiles around here.' said the policeman.
'Well, it just shows how effective it is, doesn't it.'

Gormless Gus took a friend driving on a narrow mountain road. After a while the friend said, 'I feel very scared whenever you go round one of those sharp bends.'
'Then do what I do,' said Gus, 'close your eyes.'

Inscription on the tombstone of a hypochondriac:
'I *told* you I was ill.'

One day Mr Jones came home to find
his wife wringing her hands and
weeping. 'Oh dear,' she said, 'the
cat's eaten your dinner.'
'Never mind,' he said. 'We can get a
new cat tomorrow.'

Doctor, after listening to his
patient's numerous complaints: 'I'll
write something out for you.'
Patient: Is it a prescription?
Doctor: 'No, it's a letter
of introduction to the undertaker.'

The pub beer wasn't very good. 'If
this beer had a head on it,' said a
customer, 'it would hang it in
shame.'.

Simple Simon went to buy a pillow
case. 'What size?' said the assistant.
'I don't know,' said Simon. 'But I
wear a seven-and-a-half hat.'

'Our next comedian is so bad that
when he took part in an open-air
show in the park, twenty-six trees
got up and walked out.'

Passenger: How can I make sure the
trains are running on time?
Porter: Just before one comes in, put
your watch on the line.

Jinks: I notice your neighbour doesn't let his chickens run loose any more. Why is that?
Binks: Well I hid six eggs under a bush the other night. Next day I made sure he saw me collect the eggs.

A young lady went into a bank to withdraw some money.
'Can you identify yourself?' asked the clerk.
The young lady opened her handbag, took out a mirror, looked into it and said, 'Yes, it's me all right.'

Piano Tuner: I've come to tune your piano.
Lady: But we didn't send for you.
P. Tuner: No, but your neighbours did.

Young man: I've come to ask for your daughter's hand.
Father: You'll have to take all of her, or it's no deal.

Father (at breakfast): My, son, that
was some thunderstorm we had
last night.
Son: It certainly was.
Mother: Oh dear, why didn't you
wake me up? You know I can't sleep
in a thunderstorm.

Customer: Those sausages you sent
me were meat at one end and bread
at the other.
Butcher: Yes, madam, in these
times it's difficult to make both ends
meat.

Lady: I found a fly in one of those
currant buns you sold me yesterday.
Shop owner: Well bring it back and
I'll exchange it for a currant.

Man to psychiatrist: 'I'm worried – I
keep thinking I'm a pair of
curtains:
'Stop worrying, and pull yourself
together.'

Father: When I was your age, I had
lovely wavy hair.
Son (looking at father's bald head):
Well, since then it's certainly waved
you goodbye.

'If my parents knew I was here tonight as compère they'd be ashamed – they think I'm in prison.'

Bobby had been warned to be on his best behaviour when his wealthy aunt visited. After tea, Bobby asked, 'Auntie, when are you going to do your trick?'
'What trick is that, dear?' she enquired.
'Well,' said Bobby, 'Daddy says you drink like a fish.'

Bertie: I had a trip by the seaside yesterday.
Gertie: I'm sorry to hear that – did you hurt yourself?

An Irish woman expecting her sixth child was horrified to read in her newspaper that every sixth person born in the world is Chinese.

The medical lecturer turned to one of his students and said: 'Now Merryweather, it is clear from this X-ray that one of this patient's legs is much shorter than the other. This accounts for the patient's limp. But what would *you* do in a case like this?'

Merryweather thought for a moment, then said brightly, 'Well, sir, I should imagine that I would limp too.'

Father: Well, my boy, do you think the new teacher likes you?
Jock: Oh yes, dad, she puts a wee kiss on all my sums.

Lady: What's the best way to keep fish from smelling?
Fishmonger: Just cut off their noses, lady.

Johnny: Mother, you promised to take me to see the monkeys today.
Mother: Johnny, how could you want to go and see monkeys when Grandma is here?

'Now I'd like to introduce somebody who, ten years ago, was an unknown failure. Now he's a famous failure.'

Jock: Am I your closest friend?
Duncan: I think you must be – you never give me anything.

Sammy had been on an outing with his father.
'Well,' said his mother on their return, 'did you like the zoo?'
'Oh it was fine,' replied Sammy. 'And Dad liked it too – especially when one of the animals came romping home at twenty to one.'

News broadcast: Two prisoners escaped today from Wakefield prison. One is seven feet tall and the other is four feet six. The Police are hunting high and low for them.

Overheard in Post Office.
'I want a dog licence please.'
'Yes, madam. What name?'
'Rover.'

Patient (to Psychiatrist): The trouble is, I can't help pulling funny faces.
Psychiatrist: That doesn't sound very serious.
Patient: But it's not *my* face I want to pull … it's other people's.

Brown: The police are looking for a man with one eye called Bloggs.
White: What's his other eye called?

Cloakroom attendant: Please leave your hat here, sir.
Club customer: I haven't got a hat.
Attendant: Then I'm afraid you can't come into the Club. My orders are that people cannot enter unless they leave their hat in the cloakroom.

Teacher: Order, children.
Willy: I'll have ice cream and dough-nuts.

A lady decided to breed chickens but she didn't have much luck. At last she wrote to the Ministry of Agriculture for some advice. She wrote: 'Dear Sir, Every morning I find one or two of my prize chickens lying stiff and cold on the ground with their legs in the air. Would you kindly tell me what is the matter?' A few days later she got this reply: 'Dear Madam, Your chickens are dead.'

Flora: Either the boss takes back what he said, or I walk out.
Dora: What did he say?
Flora: He told me to take a week's notice.

Office Manager: Look at all the dust on this desk. It looks as if it hasn't been cleaned for a fortnight.
Cleaning lady: Don't blame me, sir, I've only been here a week.

Father (on Jubilee Day): Where's your mother, Rosie?
Rosie: Upstairs, waving her hair.
Father: Good heavens, can't we afford a flag?

One bird to his friend: Look, there's Concorde. I wish I could go as fast as that.'
Friend bird: You could, if your bottom was on fire.

The pilot felt a gun sticking in his back, and a voice hissed in his ear: 'Take me to London.'
'But we're going to London,' said the pilot.
'I know. But I've been hi-jacked to Cuba twice before, so this time I'm taking no chances.'

Greedy Boy: I got through a jar of jam today.
Friend: From your size it must have been a tight squeeze.

'Are you trying to make a fool out of me?'
'Certainly not – why should I try to change Nature?'

'Hard lines,' said the egg in the monastery, 'Out of the frying pan into the friar.'

It was a very fancy high-class greengrocers, but the customer gasped when he was charged 75 pence for a pound of apples. He gave the girl a pound and staggered out of the shop.
'You've forgotten your change, sir,' said the girl.
'Keep it,' he said weakly. 'On my way out I trod on a grape.'

Reggie: My brother thinks he's a chicken.
Freddie: Well, why don't you take him to the doctor.
Reggie: We would, but we need the eggs.

A young man went into a pet-shop and asked for 300 beetles, 6 rats and five mice.
'I'm sorry sir,' said the petshop manager, 'but we can only supply the mice. Why do you need all the other animals?'
'I was thrown out of my flat this morning, and the landlord said I must leave the place exactly as I found it.'

'Why are you drinking blue and
white paint?'
'Because I'm an interior decorator.'

An apprentice witch-doctor was
learning the tricks of the trade from
an old witch-doctor.
Old W-D: Just watch what I do then
voo-doo the same as I do.

Old Salt: I once had a parrot for five
years and it never said a word.
Young sailor: It must have been
tongue-tied.
Old Salt: No, it was stuffed.

A worm had an invitation to a picnic
in a field of wheat. It went in one ear
and the other.

Ned: What goes ninety-nine bump,
ninety-nine bump, ninety-nine
bump?
Ed: A centipede with a wooden leg.

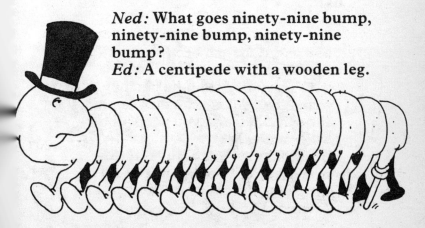

'Waiter, what soup is this?'
'It's bean soup, sir.'
'I don't want to know what it's been,
what it is now?'

Man in blood donor clinic: 'I've
come to donate a pint of blood –
where do I spit it out?'

False eyelashes are a marvellous
invention – I spent half an hour in
the bathroom trying to kill one of the
darn things.

A man bought a grandfather clock
from an antique shop. In the street
he put it over his shoulder and as he
did so knocked over an old lady.
'Idiot,' she yelled, 'who can't you
wear a wrist-watch like the rest of
us!'

Vicar: Do you say your prayers before your dinner, Pamela?
Pamela: Oh no, my mother's a good cook.

1st Businessman: My secretary has been loyal to me for years, I've seen her grow grey-headed in my service.
2nd Businessman: That's nothing; mine has been with me for three months and she's been dark brown, ash blond and now she's a red-head.

Solly: What's the weather like?
Molly: I don't know – it's so cloudy I can't see.

Grandma: I like to go to bed and get up with the chickens, don't you?
Betty: No, I like to sleep in my own bed.

Charlie: I found a horseshoe today; what do you think it means?
Dan: Perhaps the horse decided to wear socks instead.

'Why did you push her under a steamroller?'
'Because I wanted a flatmate.'

Policeman in witness box: This woman came up to me when I was in plain clothes and tried to pass off this ten pound note, m'lud.
Judge: Counterfeit?
Policeman: Yes, m'lud, she had two.

1st Pickpocket: Did you have any luck over the weekend?
2nd pickpocket: No. I spent it at a nudist camp.

> Gormless Guss walked to a rocket station and asked for a ticket to the moon. 'Sorry sir,' the gateman said, 'The moon is full.'

> *Roger:* Your overcoat is very loud.
> *Rodney:* It's not so bad when I put on a muffler.

Judge: I shall give you a short sentence.
Prisoner: Thank you, your Honour.
Judge: Ten years.
Prisoner: Ten years – that's not a short sentence!
Judge: Yes it is – – two words.

> *Doctor* (examining a patient):
> 'What's that strange growth on your head – oh, it's your head.'

Molly: Did you hear the one about the bed?
Polly: No.
Molly: It hasn't been made up yet.

'My dog plays chess with me.'
'It must be a very intelligent animal.'
'Not really. 'I've won four games out of six so far today.'

'Waiter, do you have frogs' legs?'
'Yes, sir.'
'Then leap over the counter and get me a whisky.'

A lady visiting an orchard, was amazed at the profusion of fruit, and asked the farmer: 'What do you do with all this fruit.'
'We eat what we can, and what we can't we can,' he replied.

'Waiter, there's a button in my salad.'
'Oh it must have come off when the salad was dressing.'

Stan: In his job my dad's one of the high-ups.
Dan: What does he do?
Stan: He's a steeplejack.

'Why did Lulu leave her job?'
'Illness.'
'Anything serious?'
'Yes. The boss got sick of her.'

Patient: And if I take these little blue pills as you suggested, will I get better?
Doctor: Well, put it this way; none of my patients has ever come back to ask for more.

What's the difference between an Indian elephant and an African Elephant?
– About 3,000 miles.

Waiter: We have practically everything on the menu.
Diner: So I see – would you bring me a clean one please?

Wife: I don't think I like this bananas – only diet the doctor's put me on; it seems to be having a peculiar effect on me.
Husband: Nonsense dear. Now if you'll just stop scratching yourself and come down from the curtains ...

Barry: My dad's a big time operator.
Harry: Oh, what does he do?
Barry: He winds up Big Ben.

George: I've been hunting with my pop. We brought back four rabbits and a potfer.
Joe: What's a potfer?
George: To cook the rabbits in.

Flora: I had to give up tap dancing.
Dora: Why was that?
Flora: I kept falling in the sink.

'Doctor, I feel like a pack of cards.'
'Wait over there, I'll deal with you later.'

Hetty: My doctor put me on a diet, using more corn and vegetable oils.
Betty: Does it work?
Hetty: I don't know yet – I'm no thinner, but I don't squeak any more.

Fred: What is the noblest dog?
Ned: The hot-dog – it feeds the hand that bites it.

Judge: (to Barrister): Your client doesn't seem to take the charges very seriously.
Barrister: Well, my lord, he's a professional pick-pocket, and is apt to take things rather lightly.

Sammy: (at the Fair): Who's in charge of the Nuts?
Stall-minder: Just a minute and I'll take care of you.

Customer: I'd like two pork chops,
please, and make them lean.
Butcher: Yes, madam, which way?

'This restaurant must have a very
clean kitchen.'
'Thank you, sir, how did you know?'
'Everything tastes of soap.'

Minister of Defence: a man who is
always ready to lay down *your* life
for *his* country.

Prisoner: The judge sent me here
for the rest of my life.
Governor: Have you any
complaints?
Prisoner: Well, I don't call breaking
rocks with a hammer *rest.*

Why did Moses have to be hidden
quickly when he was a baby?
Because it was a 'rush' job to save
him.

American: You English must grow awfully large.
Englishman: Why do you say that?
American: Well. I see here in the paper a woman lost five hundred pounds.

'But Cecil, it isn't our baby.'
'Shut up – it's a better pram.'

Teacher: I wish you'd pay a little attention.
Angie: I'm paying as little as I can.

After robbing the bank the thief rushed home and began to saw the legs off his bed. His wife asked him what he was doing.
'I want to lie low for a while,' he explained.

Peter: My dad makes faces all day.
Mike: Why does he do that?
Peter: He works in a clock factory.

Tommy: Jake's dad was arrested yesterday.
Timmy: Why was that?
Tommy: He went shopping after drawing twenty pounds.
Timmy: What's wrong with that?
Tommy: The drawing wasn't good enough; they spotted the forgery.

Three rather deaf old friends met
one day.
'Windy, isn't it?' said one.
'No, it's Thursday,' said the second.
'So am I,' said the third. 'Let's go and
have a cup of tea.'

'How dare you spit in front of my
wife?'
'Why, was it her turn?'

Angry man: I'll teach you to throw
stones at my greenhouse.
Little horror: I wish you would – I
keep missing it.

A visitor was being shown over a
farm, when he saw a bull in a field,
and called out: 'Is that bull safe?'
'Well,' said the farmer, 'offhand I'd
say he's a lot safer than you are.'

'I didn't come here to be insulted.'
'Why, where do you usually go?'

The German's clock would not work
properly. He prodded it, shook it,
took the back off. Finally he hissed:
'We haf vays of making you tock.'

Writer: Do you know it took me over
twenty years to find out I have no
writing ability.
Acquaintance: So what did you do –
give it up?
Writer: Oh no, by then I was so
famous I couldn't afford to.

At his execution King Charles I was
asked if he had a final request. He
said yes, he'd like to take his spaniel
for a walk around the block.

Julia: Do you like my new hair-
style?
Jack: Well, it reminds me of a
famous Italian dish.
Julia: Gina Lollobrigida?
Jack: No – spaghetti.

Mother to son: Hurry up, you'll be late for school.
Son: Don't want to go.
Mother: You must go.
Son: The teachers hate me, and the kids despise me so why should I go?
Mother: because you're forty-two years old, and you're the headmaster.

Cook: What's the best thing to put in a pie?
Maid: Your teeth.

Patient: I find it very difficult to tell the truth.
Psychiatrist: Don't worry – once you get on the couch you'll find it very hard to lie on.

'Mummy there's a man at the door with a parcel for you.
He says it's fish, and it's marked COD.'
'Well, tell him to take it back dear, I ordered haddock.'

Husband: I've just discovered oil.
Wife: Wonderful. Now we can get a new car.
Husband: We'd better get the old one fixed first – that's where the oil's coming from.

Patient: Have you got anything for
my liver, Doctor?
Doctor: Have you tried onions?

Man in sea: Help, help, I can't swim.
Drunk on shore: So what? I can't
play the violin but I'm not shouting
about it.

Teacher: If we breathe oxygen in the
daytime, what do we breathe in the
nighttime?
Margie: Nitrogen?

Lady: (dials 999): Help please come
to my house at once.
Policeman: What's the trouble,
lady?
Lady: That dreadful new postman is
sitting up in a tree in my front
garden teasing my dog.

New bridegroom: Darling, do you think you'll be able to put up with my ugly face for the rest of your life? *Bride:* I expect so, dear, you'll be out at work all day.

Man: My dog has no tail.
Friend: Then how do you know when he's happy?
Man: Oh, he stops biting me.

Ben: I hear the workers are striking for shorter hours.
Len: Good thing too – I always did think sixty minutes was too long for an hour.

Newton discovered gravity when an apple hit him on the head. He was shaken to the core.

Silly Billy came home from the railway station complaining that he felt ill because he had ridden backwards for three hours on the train.
'Why didn't you ask the person sitting opposite you to change seats?' his mother asked.
'I couldn't, he said. 'There wasn't anybody sitting opposite me.

A twenty-stone girl got engaged to a twenty-seven stone man.
They planned to have a big wedding.

'Why does Dick work in the bakery?'
'I suppose he kneads the dough.'

1st patient: I see they've brought in another case of tonsilitis.
2nd patient: Anything is better than that lousy lemonade they've been giving us lately.

'Would you like to come to my party on Saturday?'
'Yes, I'd love to. What's the address?'
'Number four New Street – just ring the bell with your elbow.'
'Why can't I ring with my finger?'
'You're not coming empty-handed, are you?'

Customer in greengrocers: One pound of mixed nuts, please – and not too many coconuts.

The absent-minded professor wished to test his class to see if they could tell the difference between a frog and a toad. But when he opened the box, he took out a sandwich. 'Good heavens,' he said, 'I could have sworn I'd just had my lunch.'

'I will now read from the Book of Numbers,' said the Vicar – and he opened the telephone directory.

The new hotel porter was being instructed by the manager, who told him always to welcome the guests by name.
'But how will I know their name?' asked the porter.
'Simple, it'll be on their case,' said the manager.
The porter was later heard saying, 'Welcome to our hotel, Mr and Mrs Simulated Leather.'

Judge: As the jury have found you Not Guilty of fraud, you are now free to go.
Prisoner: Does that mean I can keep the money?

Women are to blame for all the lying men do – they will insist on asking questions.

Pru: There are several things I can always count on.
Lou: What are they?
Pru: My fingers.

After class, the absent-minded professor asked if anybody had seen his coat.
'You have it on, sir,' he was told.
'Oh thank you very much,' he replied.
'Otherwise I might have gone off without it.'

A man bought a wristwatch and arranged to pay for it later.
He got it on tick.

A little boy noticed some green parakeets in a pet shop.
'Look mummy,' he said, 'there are some canaries that aren't ripe.'

'Gloria is the best housekeeper in the world – she's been divorced five times – and she's still got the house.'

'My wife has a slight impediment in her speech. Now and again she has to stop to take a breath.'

Mike: Does your wife cook by gas or electricity?
Jake: I don't know, I've never tried to cook her.

The creature from outer space landed in London and came upon a woman carrying a transistor. 'Earthwoman,' he said in a shocked voice, 'why do you carry your child around without clothes on?'

A policeman saw an old man pulling
a box on a lead down a busy street.
'Poor man,' he thought. 'I'd better
humour him.'
'That's a nice dog you've got there,'
he said to the old man.
'It isn't a dog, it's a box,' said the old
man.
'Oh I'm sorry,' said the policeman, 'I
thought you were a bit simple,' and
he walked on.
The old man turned and looked at
the box. 'We fooled him that time,
Rover,' he said.

Paddy asked his landlady for a full
length mirror in his room. 'You've
got a half-length mirror there now,'
she said. 'Isn't that long enough.'
'No, lady,' said Paddy. 'I've been out
three times this week without my
trousers on.'

'He's so wealthy, he bought a boy for
his dogs to play with.'

'I don't know what to buy my nephew
for his birthday.'
'Difficult – a drum takes a lot of
beating.'

Roger : My girl friend and I had a
row the other night – she wanted to
go to the ballet, and I wanted to go to
a pop concert. But we came to an
agreement.
Peter : And what was the ballet like?

Frank : Four sailors fell in the sea,
but only one of them got his hair wet.
Johnny : How was that?
Frank : Three of them were bald.

Visitor (at gate): Does your dog bite
strangers?
Man : Only when he doesn't know
them.

The professor was checking papers
in his study when his telephone rang.
His secretary answered it. 'It's a long
distance from New York,' she said.
'Yes, I know,' answered the
professor.

Customer at garage: 'I'm in a great
hurry. Don't bother with the petrol,
just give me the stamps.'

Gum Arabic: Spoken by Arabs without teeth.

'Mummy – it's getting very hot in here – can I come out?'
'Certainly not, do you want the fire to spread to the rest of the house?'

Mrs Green: I see you and your husband are taking French lessons – why is that?
Mrs Black: We've adopted a French baby and we want to be able to understand him as soon as he learns to talk.

The professor looked at one of his students: 'Haven't you a brother who took this course last year?' he asked.
'No, sir,' said the student. 'I'm just taking it again.'
'My word,' said the professor, 'Amazing resemblance.'

What did the penny say when it got stuck in the slot?
'Money's very tight these days.'

What does a Hindu? Lay eggs.

Willie: There's a black cat in the dining room, dad.
Dad: But black cats are lucky, Willie.
Willie: This one is – he's eaten your dinner.

Rory: What's in your bag?
Mike: Chickens.
Rory: Will you be giving me one of them?
Mike: No.
Rory: If I guess how many you've got then will you give me one.
Mike: Sure – if you guess correctly I'll give you both.
Rory: Six.

Two little boys were looking at an abstract painting in an art shop. 'Let's run,' said one, 'before they say we did it.'

The less people know, the more stubbornly they know it.

Sarah hadn't been paying attention when the teacher was explaining the importance of milk. When teacher asked her to name six things with milk in them she thought a moment. Then she said, 'Hot chocolate, ice-cream, rice-pudding – and three cows.'

Diner: What's the matter with this table – it's wobbling all over the place?
Waiter: The last customer spilt a bottle of wine over it, and it's still drunk.

How do we know that Moses wore a wig?
Because sometimes he was seen with Aaron and sometimes without.

Dying words of a famous Chicago gangster: 'Who put that violin in my violin case?'

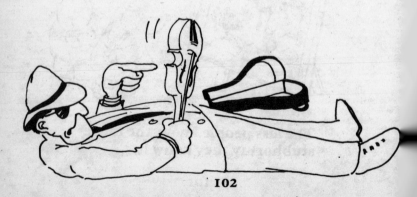

'My mother-in-law has gone to Indonesia.'
'Jakarta?'
'No – she went by plane.'

What is the difference between unlawful and illegal?
Unlawful is against the law. Illegal is a sick bird.

Ben: I saw something last night that I'll never get over.
Len: What was that?
Ben: The moon.

Ron: You dance beautifully.
Jean: I wish I could say the same for you.
Ron: You could if you were as big a liar as I am.

Tramp: I haven't had a square meal for a month, lady.
Lady: Oh you poor man – here's a dog biscuit.

Patient's brother: I'm afraid my brother thinks he's a cat.
Psychiatrist: How long has he thought that?
P's brother: Since he was a kitten.

Teacher (on phone): You say
Tommy has a cold and can't come to
school? To whom am I speaking?
Voice: This is my father.

Adam: And I shall call that creature
over there a rhinoceros.
Eve: But why call it that?
Adam: Because it looks like a
rhinoceros, stupid.

Fifi: Did you know that not all the
animals that came to Noah's Ark
came in pairs?
Bibi: Which ones didn't?
Fifi: The worms – they came in
apples.

Harry was playing the violin for his
brother. 'Well how do you like it?' he
asked.
His brother said, 'You should be on
the radio.'
'You mean I'm good enough for
that?'
'No – but then I could turn you off.'

What did Big Chief Running Water
call his two sons?
–Hot and cold.

Visitor to Zoo: Where have all the
adders gone?
Keeper: They're helping out in the
accounts department, the
computer's broken down.

Never try to drink and drive – you
might stop suddenly and spill some
of it.

The young man gave his girlfriend a
glittering necklace for her birthday.
'Ooh,' she exclaimed, 'are they real
diamonds?'
'They'd better be,' he replied, 'or I've
been swindled out of a pound.'

Teacher: Now can somebody tell me where elephants are found?
Mary: Well, elephants are so big they are hardly ever lost.

Betty: I had a fall last night which left me unconscious for eight hours.
Hetty: How dreadful! Where did you fall?
Betty: I fell asleep.

Lady on bus: Am I all right for Regents Park Zoo?
Conductor: I should think so, lady, but I'm only a conductor, not a zoologist.

The best way to make your money go further nowadays is to post it to Australia.

Frank: Am I the first man you've ever kissed?
Sue: You might be, your face looks familiar.

'What are you eating, sonny?'
'An apple.'
'Better look out for worms.'
'Let the worms look out for themselves.'

Milly: Do you have hot water at your house?
Billy: We sure do. And I'm always in it.

Holidays in Paris make you feel good enough to return to work – and so poor that you have to.

Janice: Darling, whisper something soft and sweet in my ear.
Ernest: Black forest cherry cake.

'I got a terrible fright on my wedding day.'
'Why, what happened?'
'Nothing – I married her.'

Mother: Georgie, I was hoping you would give your little brother the largest piece of cake. Even that old hen gives all the best pieces of food to her chicks, and takes only a little piece now and then for herself.
Georgie: So would I, mum, if it were worms.

Jim: I think our school must be haunted.
Tim: Why do you say that?
Jim: I'm always hearing people talk about the school spirit.

'This pair of shoes you sold me
yesterday is ridiculous.
One of them has a heel two inches
shorter than the other.
What am I supposed to do?'
'Limp.'

Waiter: And after the steak, sir,
what will you have to follow?
Diner: Indigestion, I expect.

Large Lady: I'm very annoyed with
that weighing machine.
Friend: Why's that?
Large lady: As I stepped on to it, it
said, 'One person at a time please.'

If at first you don't succeed, you're
just like 99.9 per cent of the
population.

'My uncle is a butcher, six feet tall
and wears size 12 shoes. What does
he weigh?'
'I've no idea.'
'Meat, of course.'

Visitor: And how do you like going to
school, Willie?
Willie: I like going, and I like coming
back. It's the bit in between I don't
like.

Waiter: Yes, sir, you can have
anything you see on the menu.
Diner: Well how about dirty
fingermarks, grease stains, and
gravy in that order.

Teacher: Write on one of the
following: Elizabeth the First,
Alfred the Great or John of Gaunt.
Smart Alex: I'd prefer to write on
paper.

Fat boy put a penny in the weighing
machine and stood looking at the
chart which told him how much
people of different sizes should
weigh.
After a while the chemist came out
and asked him how much he was
overweight.
'I'm not overweight,' said the Fat
boy, 'I'm just three inches too short.'

Ruby: Did you know how many sheep it takes to make one sweater?
Pearl: I didn't even know they could knit.

Teacher: At which battle did Nelson die?
Willy: His last one.

Chemistry teacher: What do you know about nitrates?
Student: Well, sir, they're a lot more expensive than day rates.

Russ: I hear your uncle was drowned in a barrel of varnish. It must have been a dreadful way to go.
Gus: Not really, he had a beautiful finish.

'You can't help admiring our boss.'
'Why is that?'
'If you don't – you're fired.'

'Do you know what C.I.D. stands for,
son?'
'Yes – Coppers in Disguise.'

To avoid that run-down feeling, look
both ways before crossing the road.

'Doctor, I was playing my flute and I
suddenly swallowed it.'
'Never mind, look on the bright side.
It could have been a grand piano.'

Gloria: Don't you feel warm doing
your painting all bundled up like
that?
Silly Sam: Well it says on the tin to
be sure to put on three coats.

A lady was horried to see a small boy
leaning against a wall smoking a
cigarette, and taking swigs from a
bottle of whisky. 'Why aren't you at
school this time of day?' she
demanded.
'School, lady,' he answered. 'Gee,
I'm only four years old.'

'My friend Dopey the Dwarf has
applied for a job in a circus.'
'Well, he should get on the short list.'

'Waiter, there's a twig in my soup.'
'Just a moment, sir, I'll call the
branch manager.'

Frank: What would I have to give
you to get a little kiss?
Za-za: Chloroform.

A man walked into the fishmongers,
and pointed to a row of trout: 'I'll
have five of these,' he said. 'But
throw them to me.'
'Why should I do that? asked the
fishmonger.
'I may be a poor fisherman,' said the
man, 'but nobody is going to call me
a liar, when I say I caught five trout.'

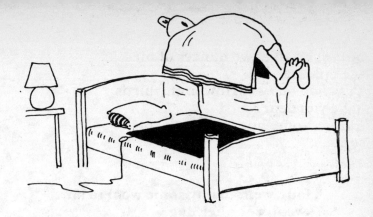

Pat: I didn't sleep well last night.
Mat: Why was that?
Pat: I plugged the electric blanket into the toaster by mistake and I kept popping out of bed all night.

Teacher: Can you tell me the difference between a buffalo and a bison?
Cockney pupil: Well you can't wash your hands in a buffalo, miss.

Jackie: I wouldn't marry you if you were the last person on earth.
Johnny: If I were, you wouldn't be here.

Mrs Higgins: I'm sorry to bring you out on such a terrible night, doctor.
Doctor: That's all right. I had to call at a house down the road, so I thought I'd kill two birds with one stone.

113

Suzie: I'd like two ounces of bird seed please.
Pet shop owner: How many birds have you dear?
Suzie: None, but I want to grow some.

A lady went to buy some wool to knit a sweater for her dog.
'Perhaps you'd better bring him in.' said the saleslady, 'then I can tell you how much wool to buy.'
'Oh no,' said the customer, 'it's supposed to be a surprise.'

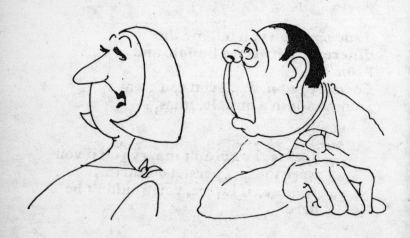

'Darling, you have the face of a saint.'
'Thank you, darling, which saint.'
'A Saint Bernard.'

The Welshman touring New York turned to his companion in the coach, a boastful American, and said: 'And where do you come from?'
'From God's own country,' replied the American.
'H'm,' said the Welshman, 'then you've got a very poor Welsh accent.'

'Your money or your life,' said the hold-up man to the miser. When there was no reply, he repeated the demand:
'Come on, man, your money or your life, which is it to be?'
'Quiet,' said the miser, 'I'm thinking about it.'

Patrick: Did you mark that place on the water where the fishing is so good?
Mike: Course I did. I put a cross on the side of the boat.
Patrick: Idiot – we might get another boat next time.

Walter: A steam-roller ran over my uncle.
Richard: What did you do?
Walter: I took him home and slipped him under the door.

Larry: It's raining cats and dogs today.
Carry: I know – I've just stepped into a poodle.

Post Office clerk: You've addressed this letter upside down.
Paddy: That's right – it's going to Australia.

Lady: Can this wool coat be worn in wet weather?
Assistant: Madam, have you ever seen a sheep carry an umbrella?

A man and his wife were looking over a house. The estate agent said to them: 'It's only a stone's throw from the bus stop.'
'We'll take it,' said the man. 'There'll always be something to do in the evening, throwing stones at buses.'

'You can't say my husband is two-
faced – or he wouldn't wear that one
all the time.'

Yesterday three Irishmen hi-jacked
a submarine, and then demanded a
million pounds – and three
parachutes.

Teacher: You missed school
yesterday, didn't you Sammy?
Sammy: Not much miss.

A man came to the police station and
complained: 'I've got three brothers
– we all live in one room. One of my
brothers has six cats, another has
five dogs, and the other has a goat.
The smell is terrible. Can you do
something about it?'
'Well, why don't you open the
windows?' asked the policeman.
'What, and lose all my pigeons,' said
the man.

Angie: How are you getting on
teaching Charlie to dance?
Rosie: Well I'm hoping soon he'll be
able to stand on his own feet instead
of mine.

Bernie: How are you getting on in your new ten-roomed house?
Barney: Not too badly. We furnished the living room by collecting cornflakes packets.
Bernie: What about the other rooms?
Barney: We can't do them yet – they're full of cornflakes.

Buster: What are you doing?
Goofy: Writing a letter to my brother.
Buster: But you can't write.
Goofy: That doesn't matter. My brother can't read.

The mother kangaroo leapt into the air with a cry of pain.
'Joey,' she said, 'how many more times do I have to tell you not to smoke in bed.'

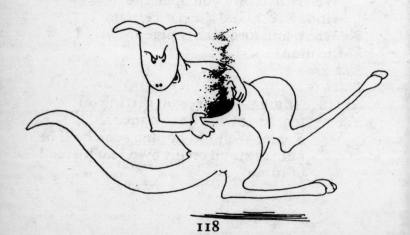

Norman: You remind me of the sea.
Gloria: Why, because I'm so wild,
reckless and romantic?
Norman: No – you make me sick.

Percival was so wealthy that even
the bags under his eyes had his
initials on them.

'Doctor, you remember last year you
told me to stay away from dampness
if I wanted my rheumatism to get
better?'
'Yes,' said the doctor.
'Well, it's better. Is it all right for me
to take a bath now?'

Cyclist: My bike's always going
wrong. I think it must have a jinx.
Friend: Yes, it's probably put a
spook in your wheel.

Val (answering phone) Hello.
Voice: Hello. Is Boo there?
Val: Boo who?
Voice: Don't cry little girl. I must
have the wrong number.

What are government workers
called in Seville?
Seville servants.

The first Welsh milkman put up a sign over his shop saying 'Idris Evans – Dairy'. The second Welsh milkman put up a sign saying 'Evans – best dairy goods.' The third Welsh milkman put up a smaller notice, saying 'Evans the Milk – Main Entrance.'

A novice at the stables was trying to saddle a horse.
'Excuse me,' said the old hand, 'but you're putting that saddle on backwards.'
'How do you know,' snapped the novice. 'You don't know which way I'm going.'

Pat and Mike each kept a horse in the same field. In order to tell which was which they tied a green ribbon on Pat's horse. One day the ribbon fell off.
'How shall we tell which is which now?' asked Pat.
'I know,' said Mike, 'you take the brown one, and I'll have the white one.'

Fred: I hear your wife's a poor driver.
Ned: Yes – even the lights go white when they see her coming.

Keep smiling – it makes everyone
wonder what you're up to.

Tourist: Whose skull is that one?
Tired guide: That, sir, is the skull of
Julius Caesar.
Tourist: Then whose is that small
one beside it?
Guide: That, sir, is the skull of Julius
Caesar when he was a small boy.

A man in an agitated state rushed
into a pub. 'Has anybody here got a
large black cat with a white collar?'
he asked.
Nobody answered. He tried again.
'Does anybody have a large black cat
with a white collar?' But still nobody
answered.
'Oh dear,' he murmured. 'I must
have run over the vicar.'

Sergeant: Let's get our bearings.
You're facing north; west is on your
left, and east is on your right.
What's at your back?
Private: My knapsack.

"I've made the chicken soup.'
'Good – I was afraid it was for us.'

Teacher: Your hands are very dirty,
Sidney. What would you say if I
came with dirty hands?
Sidney: I'd be too polite to mention
it.

'I understand you buried your
husband last week?'
'Yes – I had to; he was dead.'

Water Bailiff: Young lady, I have to
arrest you for swimming in this
river here.
Young Lady: But surely you could
have told me before I changed into
my swim suit.
Bailiff; There's no law against *that*,
my dear.

Cannibal (to his daughter): Now you
are old enough to get married, we
must look around for an edible
bachelor.

Post-office clerk: Here's your ten pence stamp.

Shopper (with arms full of shopping): Do I have to stick it on myself?

Post-office clerk: No. On the envelope.

If you sat in a bucket of glue, would you have a sticky end?

The census-taker knocked on Miss Matty's door. She answered all his questions except her age. She refused to tell him this.

'But everybody tells their age to the census-taker,' he said.

'Did Miss Maisie Hill and Miss Daisy Hill tell you their ages?'

'Certainly.'

'Well I'm the same age,' she snapped.

'As old as the Hills,' he wrote on his form.

Effie: My auntie was very embarrassed when she was asked to take off her mask at the party.
Tessie: Why was that?
Effie: She wasn't wearing one.

'Are you a mechanic?'
'No, I'm a Mactavish.'

'I can't understand how those bank robbers got away,' said the Constable. 'Were all the exits guarded?'
'Certainly, sir'.
'Well, they must have gone out by the entrance.'

'I've just bought a suit that fits me like a glove.'
'You must be very pleased.'
'Not really – four trouser legs and one sleeve.'

An ambulance man arriving at the hospital saw two doctors searching in the flower-beds. 'Excuse me,' he said, 'have you lost something?' 'No,' replied one, 'we're doing a heart transplant for a tax inspector, and we're looking for a suitable stone.'

Tess: They call him the wonder boy.
Bess: Why is that?
Tess: They look at him and wonder.

Think of a number between one and twenty. Double it, subtract eighteen, add one, subtract the number you started with, close your eyes ....
Dark, isn't it!

Pete: My wife converted me to religion?
Stan: How did she do that?
Pete: I didn't believe in Hell until I married her!

Hold-up man: Will you give me your
money or shall I shoot you?
Bert: Shoot me. I need the money
for my old age.

What did the traffic lights say to the
sports car?
–Don't look now, I'm changing.

Husband (to wife who is slimming)
Don't you find it hard to go without
sugar?
Wife: No, when I think about it a
lump just comes into my throat.

Little girl: I was going to buy you
some hankies for Christmas, Uncle,
but I couldn't remember the size of
your nose.

Dorothy: I'm not going to school
any more.
Mother: Why ever not?
Dorothy: On Monday teacher said
five and five makes ten. On Tuesday
she said six and four makes ten.
Today she said seven and three
makes ten. 'I'm not going back till
she makes up her mind.

Maisie: What did one tonsil say to the other tonsil?
Daisy: I don't know, what?
Maisie: Get dressed. Doctor is taking us out tonight.

Martin: Why do doctors and nurses wear masks?
Mike: So that if someone makes a mistake, no one will know who did it.

What happened to the cat who swallowed a ball of wool?
–She had mittens.

An Irishman bought a pair of water skis – now he's looking for water with a slope.

John: Why is Sunday the strongest day?
Joan: Because all the others are *week*days.

Jackson: There's one word that describes my wife – temperamental.
Jones: In what way?
Jackson: She's fifty per cent temper and fifty per cent mental!

The home team had been beaten ten nil and trooped sadly back to the dressing room. 'Cheer up, boys,' said the manager, 'at least you won something, even if it was only the toss.'

Stan: What are you taking for your cold?
Sid: What will you give me?

The cow slipped and fell on the ice. But little Audrey laughed and laughed – she knew it was no use crying over spilt milk.

'Where did I come from?' asked the baby ear of corn.
'The stalk brought you,' answered its mother.

'I wouldn't say my boss has a big mouth but he called me from London yesterday. I was in Birmingham, and we don't have a telephone.'

Husband (phoning his wife from his office): I've got two tickets for the ballet.
Wife: Oh, lovely, I'll start getting ready.
Husband: Yes, do – the tickets are for tomorrow night.

Teacher: Jimmy, can you tell me a common use for cow-hide?
Jimmy: Well, to hold the cows together.

Bert had a letter from his mother. 'Dear Bert, so much has happened since you were home. I've had all my teeth out, and a new gas-stove put in …'

'Why do you call your wife Camera –
that can't be her real name?'
'No – her real name's Iris, but I call
her Camera because she's always
snapping at me.'

The little girl had jelly in one ear and
custard in the other. An old lady
asked her what she was doing with
jelly in one ear and custard in the
other.
'You'll have to speak up,' said the
little girl, 'I'm a trifle deaf.'

Phil: Where did he meet her?
Bill: They met in a revolving door,
and he's been going round with her
ever since.

Teacher: Can anyone tell me what
sort of insect a slug is?
Aleck: Yes, sir – a snail with a
housing problem.

Young Larry and Barry were
watching men on high scaffolding
repairing a tall chimney.
'What would you do if you were up
there and that thing fell?' Larry
asked.
'I would wait until it got nearly to the
ground and then I would jump.'

When Buster was born they fired twenty-one guns. Unfortunately they all missed.

'Excuse me, can you tell me the time?'
'I'm sorry – I'm a stranger here myself.'

Know-all Agricultural Student: Your methods seem very out of date here: I'd be surprised if you could get ten pounds of apples out of that tree.
Farmer: So would I – it's a peach tree.

The vacancy is for a litter-collector. Have you any experience?
–No, but I'll pick it up as I go along.

Sunday School teacher: And what is the Holy See of Rome?
Little Myra: It's when the Pope looks at himself in a mirror.

Boy from City: Why are you ploughing your field with a steam roller?
Farmer: I'm growing mashed potatoes this year.

Mother: How did you get Wayne to take his medicine without protest?
Father: I shot it into him with a water pistol.

Phil: Why is it dangerous to tell a secret on a farm?
Bill: I don't know. Why?
Phil: Because the potatoes have eyes, the corn have ears, and the beans talk.

Teacher: I hope I didn't see you looking at someone else's paper Jamie.
Jamie: I hope so too, teacher.

'My uncle gets a warm reception wherever he goes.'
'He must be very popular.'
'No, he's a fireman.'

132

Teacher: Do you know that Russell boy?
Principal: What about him?
Teacher: Not only is he the worst-behaved child in the school, but he has a perfect attendance record.

Ted: I have in my hand two coins – which total fifty-five pence. One is not a five-pence piece. What are the two coins?
Fred: I've no idea.
Ted: One is a fifty pence piece – the *other* is five-pence.

Teacher: What is a skeleton?
Mervyn: It's a man with his outsides off and his insides out.

It was the old missionary in Africa who gave the cannibals their first taste of Christianity.

Bud: I can find my wife anywhere I go.
Bill: How?
Bud: I just open my wallet, and there she is.

Vicar: (talking about the changing fashions of the day) It's certainly made a change to the collection.
Verger: Yes and since zips came in we get fewer buttons on the plate.

Smith: You seem to have been working in your garden. Mr Brown – what are you growing?
Brown: Tired.

Algy: What kind of paper should I use for my kite?
Reggie: What about fly-paper!

Mother: How did my best vase get broken?
Son: I was cleaning my catapult and it went off.

A lady dropped her umbrella over the edge of the platform at Paddington Station. The porters refused to retrieve it as they considered it beneath their station.

Percy received a letter from his wife:
'Dear Percy, I missed you yesterday. Please come home again and let me have another shot.'

Mabel: You must have paid the earth for that coat.
Jessie: No, I got it dirt cheap.

Willie: What is frozen tea?
Sammy: Iced tea.
Willy: What is frozen beer?
Sammy: Iced beer.
Willy: What is frozen ink?
Sammy: Iced ink?
Willy: Well, go and have a bath.

Dan: This match won't light.
Stan: Why, what's the matter with it?
Dan: I don't know – it was alright a minute ago.

Teacher: Now, Jane, your sister gave me exactly the same essay on your holiday picnic!

Jane: Well, miss, it was the same picnic.

Patient: Tell me straight, doctor, how long have I got?

Doctor: It's difficult to say, but if I were you I wouldn't start reading any serials.

Vi: Is it true you married Joe for the money his grandfather left him?

Di: Certainly not! I'd have married him whoever had left him money.

Maths teacher: If the average car is ten feet long, and if a million cars were placed end to end –

Graham: It would be August Bank Holiday on the way to Brighton.

Policeman: After the way you've been driving, I shall now introduce you to Eliza.
Motorist: Who's Eliza?
Policeman: Breath-eliza.

A man was seen on a park bench today dressed only in a newspaper. He said he liked to dress with The Times.

Bob: What inventions have helped me to get up in the world?
Ben: I don't know, which?
Bob: The lift, the escalator and the alarm clock.

Salesman: Would you like to try our new oatmeal soap?
Lady: No, thank you, I never wash my oatmeal.

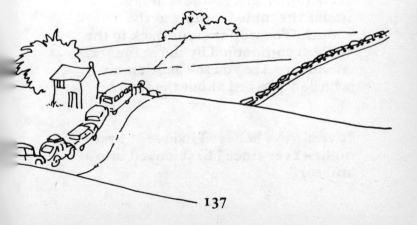

Priest (visiting Paddy in hospital):
Now, Paddy, I shall pray for you to
forgive O'Toole for hitting you on
the head with that bottle.
Paddy: Don't bother, Father, wait
till I come out of here and then you
can pray for O'Toole.

Teacher: Where was the Magna
Carta signed?
Dolly: At the bottom, miss.

Attendant at Lost Property Office:
Oh no – first you tell me what you've
lost, and then I tell you what we've
got.

Father: I'm worried about you
always being at the bottom of your
class.
Freddie: Don't worry, dad. They
teach the same thing at both ends.

A customer in a restaurant lay
under the table foaming at the
mouth. The waiter came back to the
table accompanied by the manager.
Manager: Are you the gentleman
who complained about the food?

'I've always believed in love at first
sight – ever since I first looked into a
mirror.'

Johnny: Hey, mum, the old clothes man's here.
Mum: No, Johnny, we have plenty of old clothes.

Cannibal to Missionary: Well, if God didn't intend you to be eaten, why did he make you out of meat?

Christine made her husband a millionaire.
Before she married him he was a multi-millionaire.

Morris: I hear the workers in the Mint are complaining of having too much work to do.
Harris: Yes, they're threatening to come out on strike unless they make less money.

A Frenchman jumped into a very long river in Paris yesterday. He was reported to be In Seine.

Teacher: Yes, Nigel, what is it?
Nigel: I don't want to alarm you, miss, but my Dad said if I didn't get better marks someone was going to get a licking.

Hickory dickory dock
Three mice ran up the clock
The clock struck one
But the other two managed to get away!

Teacher: Without oxygen, human life would not be possible. This important gas was discovered in 1773.
Godfrey: Miss, what did people breathe before oxygen was discovered?

Pretty girl at party to Best-selling author: Oh I've read all your books – the one I liked best was the one with the green leather cover and the gold lettering ...

Overheard at Magicians' Convention: 'Hi there, Terry, how's tricks?'

Paddy was stopped at the Customs. 'What's in this bottle?' asked the Customs officer.
'Sure, an' it's Holy Water from Lourdes,' said Paddy.
The Customs Officer didn't believe him and tasted it.
'It looks like whisky, it smells like whisky, and it tastes like whisky,' he said sternly.
'Glory be,' said Paddy – 'another miracle'.

Algernon Smythe-Brown: (to Bertie Billings) 'I bet my father has a higher mortgages repayment than your father.'

'I won't say my parents don't like me, but when I got home from school last week, they'd moved house.'

Upright citizen: You should pay your taxes with a smile.
Friend: Yes, I'd like to, but they insist on cash.

Doctor: How are you now, Mr Gibson, after your heart operation?
Mr Gibson: Well, doctor, I seem to have two heartbeats.
Doctor: Oh dear, I wondered where my wristwatch had gone.

Mavis: I'm thinking of divorcing Jeff, he smokes in bed.
Belle: But surely that's not sufficient reason?
Mavis: The trouble is he smokes kippers.

Ted: My dad's played at Wembley lots of times.
Ned: I didn't know he was a footballer.
Ted: He isn't. He plays in a brassband.

After being unconscious for twenty-four hours Shaun turned to see his friend Paddy just stirring at his side. 'What happened?' said Shaun.
'I don't know,' said Paddy. 'The last thing I remember thinking was how could they sell it for 75p a bottle.'

Voice on phone: Is that the Game Warden?
Game Warden: Yes, sir.
Voice: Oh, could you please suggest some games for my boy's birthday party?

The lady with the large flowery hat was stopped at the church door by the usher:
'Are you a friend of the bride?' he asked.
'Certainly not,' she snapped. 'I'm the bridegroom's mother.'

143

'Oh Doctor, I've swallowed the film
out of my camera.'
'Well we'll just have to hope that
nothing develops.'

Notice on Street Vendor's barrow:
CAMERAS AS ADVERTISED ON
POLICE 5.

Overheard at Nudist colony:
'Oh I didn't recognise you in glasses,
Mr Ormrod – you look
so intellectual.'

Mrs White: And where are you
living now, Mrs Green.
Mrs Green: Just by the river – drop
in some time.

Henry: This old tramp came up to
me and said he hadn't had a bite in
two weeks.
Bob: Poor chap – what did you do?
Henry: Bit him of course!

Mrs O: I bought a second hand
carpet in mint condition.
Mrs C: How could that be?
Mrs O: It had a hole in the middle.

'I think grandma needs new glasses?'
'What makes you say that, son?'
'She's been watching two pairs of
father's trousers going round in the
washing machine – and thinks she's
watching a wrestling match on telly'

Football Manager: You played a
great game there, Edwards.
Edwards: Oh sir, I thought I played
rather badly.
Manager: No, you played a great
game for the other side.

Mo: Where do you weigh whales?
Jo: I don't know.
Mo: At a whale weigh station.

Mother: Eat your cabbage dear, it
will put colour into your cheeks.
Angie: Who wants green cheeks.

'What's a girl like you doing in a nice place like this?'

Barber (to youth with slick plastered-down hair): Do you just want me to cut it or would you like an oil check too?

The man in the front row of the cinema was making loud groaning noises while tender scenes were being played on the screen.
After repeated attempts to 'hush' him the manager was sent for. 'Get up!' demanded the manager.
'Oooooooaaaaaggg' shouted the man.
'Where are you from?' asked the manager.
'From … the … balcony … ' gasped the man.

Office Manager: I'm afraid that young man I hired isn't honest.
Accounts clerk: Oh, you shouldn't judge by appearance.
Office Manager: I'm not – I'm judging by disappearance.

Roger: Do you know why Eskimos eat candles?
Reggie: No, why?
Roger: For light refreshment.

The navvies went on strike because of the new mechanical shovel. It was too dangerous to lean on.

'My wife is so fat that when I married her, to carry her over the threshold I had to make two trips.'

George: I see you're still on crutches old lad?
Desmond: Yes – that's the last time I'll try and jump over the net at table tennis.

Judge: I don't understand why you broke into the same store three nights in a row?
Prisoner: Well, your Honour, I picked out a dress for my wife, and I had to change it twice.

Auntie: Well, Gordon, suppose there were only two pieces of cake left – a large piece and a small one. Which piece would you give to your brother?
Gordon: Do you mean my big brother or my little one?

Receptionist: Doctor Chaunchadinjhi is waiting for you sir?
Patient: Which doctor?
Receptionist: Oh no, he's fully qualified.

Simon: Which side of the bed do you sleep on?
Dopey Dan: The top side, of course.

'I heard footsteps and got out of bed, and then there was a tap on my door.'
'Heavens, what a funny place for a tap.'

'Why don't you answer the
telephone?'
'It's not ringing.'
'Oh you always have to leave
everything till the last minute.'

The muddled old gentleman went up
to another man at the conference. 'I
hardly recognised you,' he said.
'You've changed so much; your hair
is different, you seem shorter, you've
done away with your glasses. What's
happened to you, Mr Frost?'
   'But I'm not Mr Frost.'
'Amazing – you've even changed
your name.'

'And how do you like the meat balls?'
'I don't know – I've never been to
any.'

Little Diana was standing in front of
her mirror with her eyes closed.
'Why are you standing there with
your eyes closed?' asked her brother.
'So I can see what I'm like when I'm
asleep,' she replied.

Man in tie store: Could you let me
have a tie that would match my eyes,
please?
Lady assistant: I'm afraid they
don't make them in bloodshot tone,
sir.

149

Dug: What do you think happened to the plant in our arithmetic class?

Reg: I don't know, what?

Dug: It grew square roots.

Tailor: Your suit will be ready in two months sir.

Customer: Two months. But it only took six days when God made the world.

Tailor: True, sir. But look at the state the world is in.

Maud: Samantha reminds me of a film star.

Ivy: Really – which one?

Maud: Lassie.

Voice on phone: Is Mr Miller in yet?

Secretary: No, he hasn't even been in yesterday yet.

Hoh Chang: I like velly much the flute.

English Host: And do you play it?

Hoh Chang: Play it? No, I eat it – apples, bananas – pears.

Teacher: Are you sure that's your mother's signature on this excuse-note?

Ronnie: Oh yes, miss – here's the tracing to prove it.

Patient: I always feel that I'm covered in gold paint, doctor.

Psychiatrist: Oh that's just a gilt complex.

'I think I've got measles.'

'That's a rash thing to say.'

Molly: That's a nice suit you're wearing.

Harry: Oh, do you like it?

Molly: Yes, who went for the fitting?

Student: Did you say you learned to play the violin in six easy lessons?

Master: That's right. It was the seven hundred that came afterwards that were the hard ones.

Simple Simon: I've been feeling run down doctor and I've been taking the vitamin pills, but they don't seem to do me any good.
Doctor: Perhaps it's your diet. What have you been eating?
Simple Simon: Oh, are you supposed to eat as well?

Julie: That boy's annoying me.
Wendy: Why, he's not even looking at you.
Julie: I know, that's what's annoying me.

Clare: I see you are invited to Sandra's party?
Zoë: Yes, but I can't go. The invitation says 4 to 7, and I'm eight.

Father: What's that gash on your forehead?
Silly son: I bit myself.
Father: How on earth could you do that?
Silly son: I stood on a chair.

Teacher: Wendy, say something beginning with 'I',
Wendy: 'I is …'
Teacher: No, Wendy, you must say I'm …'
Wendy: All right, I am the ninth letter of the alphabet.

'My sister married an Irishman.'
'Oh really?'
'No, O'Grady.'

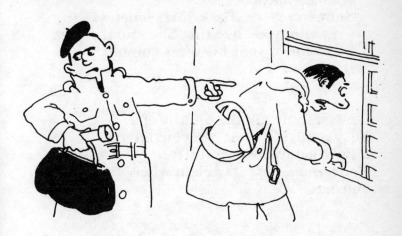

Thief: Quick – the police are coming
– jump out of the wondow!
Accomplice: But we're on the
thirteenth floor.
Thief: This is no time to be
superstitious.

'Waiter, this coffee tastes like mud.'
'Well, sir, it was ground only five
minutes ago.

'How did you get the puncture?'
'Ran over a milk bottle.'
'But didn't you see it?'
'No – a kid had it hidden under his
coat.'

Percy's mother was worried about the health of her neighbour.
'Percy,' she said, 'run and ask how old Mrs Jones is.'
Soon Percy was back. 'Mrs Jones was very annoyed.' he said. 'She said it was none of your business how old she is.'

Girl (standing in the middle of a busy road): Officer, can you tell me how to get to the hospital?
Policeman: Just stay right where you are.

Did you hear about the cross-eyed teacher?
He couldn't control his pupils.

Man (teaching his wife to drive): I implore you, if you can't control it, at least run it into something cheap.

During a violent storm, an old man fell down in the street, and was dying when help reached him. 'Get me a rabbi,' he pleaded, 'I'm dying'.
'What's your name?'
'Patrick O'Grady. Get me a rabbi.'
'Surely you mean a priest.'
'Not at all – I wouldn't fetch the priest out on a night like this.'

A lady went to visit a friend and carried a small box with holes punched in the top.
'What's in your box?' asked the friend.
'A cat,' said the lady. 'You see I've been dreaming about mice at night, and I'm so scared, this cat is to catch the.'
'But the mice are only imaginary,' said the friend.
'So is the cat,' whispered the lady.

Mother: Shall I put the kettle on?
Father: No, dear, I don't think it would suit you.

Albert: Darling, when we are married do you think you will be able to live on my income?
Una: I think so, darling, but what will you live on?

Eric: I've been asked to get married
hundreds of times.
Gloria: (surprised): Who by?
Eric: My parents.

Did you hear about the man who was
so mean he fired a revolver outside
his house on Christmas Eve then
went inside and told his children that
Father Christmas had committed
suicide.

A motorist driving through the
Cotswolds wasn't sure he was on the
right road, and stopped his car to ask
a farmer in a tractor. 'Which way is
it to Cheltenham?' he asked.
'Don't know,' said the farmer.
'Well which way is it to Cirencester?'
'Don't know.'
'Don't you know anything?'
'Well,' said the farmer, 'I ain't lost.'

Roger: Don't you find it sticky
travelling to town these days?
Monty: Yes – it's jam all the way.

Scientist (at Scientific congress)
Gentlemen, we have now discovered
an acid that will eat up everything.
Voice from the floor: What are we
going to keep it in?

Clever Dick (to shoe salesman): How
much are your ten pound shoes?
Salesman: Five pounds a foot, sir.

'I've got a nasty pain in my right
foot, doctor.'
'I shouldn't worry – it's just old age.'
'Well, why doesn't the other one hurt
– I've had that just as long.'

Bertie: I got 100 in biology today,
and still didn't pass.
Father: (horrified) Why ever not?
Bertie: The answer was 200.

Two ears of corn ran up a hill. What
were they when they reached the
top?
Puffed Wheat.

Man in restaurant: Excuse me, waiter, how long have you been working here?
Waiter: About two months, sir.
Man: Oh, then it couldn't have been you who took my order.

Sheila: I bumped into Betty today.
Frank: Was she pleased to see you?
Sheila: Not really – we were both in our cars at the time.

Jesse James and his faithful steed Bronco were ambushed by a band of Apache. 'Well, ol' friend,' said Jesse – 'this looks like curtains for both of us.'
Bronco looked at his master – 'What do you mean *both* of us, White man!'

'Why are you so angry?'
'Well, it's all the rage.'

Physics teacher: Is there any difference between lightning and electricity?
Smart Alec: Yes – you don't have to pay for lightning.

Eric: When they take out your appendix, it's an appendectomy; when they take your tonsils out it is a tonsillectomy.
What is it when they remove a growth from your head?
Derrick: I don't know.
Eric: A hair-cut.

Penny: What do you think of the new vicar?
Bonny: Quite good – I didn't know much about sin until he came.

Jeff: Why are you standing in that bowl of water?
Goofy: The tablets I'm taking say 'To be taken in water three times a day.'

I stayed on a farm and one day a chicken died, so we had roast chicken. The next day a pig died and we had pork chops. The following day the farmer died – so I left.

'Mummy, we're pretending to be
elephants at the zoo. Will you help
us?'
'Of course, dear. What am I to do?'
'Well, you're the lady who feeds us
buns.'

Rosie: This ointment makes my leg
smart.
Rob: Well why not rub some on your
head!

When I started courting my wife, she
made me lay all my cards on the
table – Barclaycard, Access,
American Express.

Wife (to motorist husband): I could
do with a nice cup of tea.
Husband: Well we'd better look for a
'T' junction.

Charlie (in the bank): Has anyone dropped a wad of notes? Several people called out, 'Yes, I did.'
Charlie: Well I've just found the rubber band.

Patient: Doctor, do you think lemons are healthy?
Doctor: Well, I've never heard one complain.

Harry's girlfriend refused to marry him because of religious differences. He was poor and she worshipped money.

Two little girls in Hollywood were talking.
Samantha: What's your new daddy like?
Christine: Oh he's okay. Have you met him?
Samantha: Yes, we had him last year.

Paula: Why are you plugging your
guitar into the lamp standard?
Peter: I like light music.

The doctor came to remove the
plaster cast from the old lady's leg.
'What a relief,' she said.'Now can I
climb stairs again?'
'Of course,' said the doctor.
'That's good,' said the old lady.
'You've no idea what a job it was
shinning up and down that
drainpipe.'

'How much is that bird?'
'Three pounds, sir.'
'I'll have it. Will you send me the
bill?'
'I'm sorry, sir, you'll have to take the
whole bird.'

'Did you hear the one about the piece
of rope?'
'No.'
'Aw, skip it.'

The show-off at the party was at it
again.
'What's he doing now?' asked Brown.
'Oh, he's doing his impression of a
river,' said Jones.
'Small at the head and big at the
mouth.'

Spike: Why is your dog running around in circles?
Mike: He's a watchdog, and he's winding himself.

Andy: What's the best thing to take when you are run down?
Sandy: The number of the car that hit you.

Steve: What kind of a dog is that?
Stan: It's a police dog.
Steve: It doesn't look like one.
Stan: Of course not. He's in the secret service.

Mayor (to Visitor): What do you think of our town band?
Visitor: I think it ought to be.
Mayor (puzzled): Ought to be what?
Visitor: Banned.

Barry: I wish I had enough money to buy an aeroplane.
Garry: What do you want an aeroplane for?
Barry: I don't. I just wish I had that much money.

Little Diana: Can you stand on your head?
Lulu: No, I can't get my feet up high enough.

Vic: I've changed my mind.
Dick: Thank goodness. Does the new one work any better?

Jackson: Why do you have two 'L' plates on your car?
Johnson: One is for my wife who's learning to drive – the other is for her mother in the back who's learning to be a back-seat driver.

164

Two ladies met after a long time.
Mrs Hughes: I believe your son is a
very good football player. What
position does he play?
Mrs Evans: Oh, I believe he's one of
the drawbacks.

The judge was only 4 feet 2 inches
tall.
–A little thing sent to try us.

Teacher: Hands up all those who
wish to go to Heaven. All the
children put up their hands, except
for little Barbara.
Teacher: Barbara, don't you want to
go to Heaven?
Barbara: Well, miss, me mum said I
had to go straight home after school.

Teacher: Now, Willie, if you bought
fifty apples for ten pence what would
each one be?
Willie: Rotten – at that price they'd
have to be.

Owner of rather decrepit hotel: Yes,
we have a room, but you'd have to
make your own bed.
Desperate traveller: That's okay.
Owner of Hotel: Right – there's a
hammer, and saw, and some nails.

Young angler: Is this a good river
for fish?
Old Angler: It must be – I can't get
any of them to come out.

Brown: Green stole a calendar.
What do you think the judge gave
him?
White: Twelve months.

Do twins born in Amsterdam speak
Double Dutch?

Auntie: Well, Billy, how do you like
school?
Billy: Closed.

Dicky: Stan reminds me of a fence.
Micky: What makes you say that?
Dicky: He runs around a lot but
never gets anywhere.

The science class had been asked to
write a five-page essay on nutrition.
When Barney handed in his essay the
teacher said, 'But I asked for five
pages – and you've only done one
page.'
'I know, said Barney. 'I was writing
about condensed milk.'

'Charlie,' called out the news editor to his cub reporter, 'did you get that story about the man who sings tenor and baritone at the same time?' 'There's no story, sir,' said the reporter. 'The man has two heads.'

'Can I buy a television licence for half-price?'
'Certainly not – why should you?'
'Well, I can only see with one eye.'

'Do you sell dog's meat?'
'Only if they come with their owners.'

Vic: She sure gave you a dirty look.
Dick: Who?
Vic: Mother Nature!

A large hole was discovered in the walls surrounding the Carefree Nudist Camp at Brownham-on-Sea. The police are looking into it.

The Income Tax inspector had been visiting the school to talk about taxes. 'I'm going to tell you now about indirect taxes. Can anybody tell me what an indirect tax is?' 'A dog licence' said Smart Alec. 'Why is that?' asked the Inspector. 'The dog doesn't pay it.'

Mrs Grabbit: Darling, the woman next door has a coat exactly like mine.
Mr Grabbit: I suppose that's a hint that you want a new coat?
Mrs Grabbit: Well, it would be cheaper than moving house.

Father (going through his morning mail): I see Mrs Simpkins has notified us of her change of address.
Mother: She's lucky – it's years since I've had a change of a dress.

'My brother's so mean – he promised me a food mixer for a wedding present, and when it came I opened the parcel and there it was – a wooden spoon.'

Bossy lady: I throw myself into everything I undertake.
Fed-up neighbour: Well, why not go and dig a deep well.

Mr Ward: Doctor says I must get rid of twenty pounds.
Mr Ward: I'll help you dear. I'll go out and buy a new dress and you'll get rid of twenty pounds in no time.

Benjie was sent to the greengrocers
for three pounds of bananas. After
he came home his mother phoned
the shop and complained, 'I sent my
son for three pounds of bananas
and you've only given him two.'
'Madam,' said the shopkeeper, 'my
scales are correct. Have you weighed
your son?'

'My wife is so thin when she goes to
the park, the ducks throw her bread.'

Goofy's mother told him to get out of
the house – and suggested he go
window-shopping.
He did, and came back with five
windows.

Leslie: Did your mother go in for
weight-lifting?
Wesley: No, why?
Leslie: Well, how did she ever raise a
dumb–bell like you?

Tony: Where do you have the longest
view in the world?
Tim; I've no idea. Where?
Tony: By a roadside where there are
telephone poles, because then you
can see from pole to pole.

Teacher: What did James Watt do when he saw steam coming from the kettle?

Bright boy: He decided to make a nice cup of tea.

'Waiter, there's a fly in my soup.'
'If you throw it a pea it will play water polo.'

Mother: Where are you off to, Hubert?

Hubert: I'm going to watch a solar eclipse.

Mother: Alright, dear, but don't get too close.

Vera: Is your electric toaster a pop-up?

Val: No, it's a Red Indian model.

Vera: What's that?

Val: It sends up smoke signals.

171

Phil: My girlfriend's like the back of a watch.
Bill: What do you mean?
Phil: She's always behind time.

'Why does George work as a baker?'
'To earn an honest crust.'

A little boy at the seaside saw a beautiful new Rolls Royce parked on the promenade, and with his metal-ended spade he scratched several lines across its side. His father, who was following him, clouted him. 'What have I told you,' he said. 'If you break that spade, you won't get another one.'

A baby mouse saw a bat for the first time. He ran home yelling, 'Mummy, mummy, I've just seen an angel.'

Effie and George had been going steady for thirty-five years. One day after reading a love-story, Effie said, 'Let's get married, George.'
'Don't be silly,' said George. 'Who'd marry us at our time of life?'

Steve: I think dentists must be very unhappy at their work.
Dave: Why do you think so?
Steve: Well, they always look down in the mouth.

Mother: When that horrid boy threw stones at you, you should have come to me instead of throwing them back at him.
Jimmy: What good would that do? You can't hit the side of a house.

Teacher: If you washed cars for twenty people and they each gave you twenty pence, what would you get?
Gilbert: A new bicycle.

Policeman (apprehending a burglar): Anything you say may be held against you.
Burglar: Miss World.

173

Artist: You're the first model I've ever kissed.
Model: I bet you say that to all your models. How many have you had?
Artist: Well, there was a vase of flowers, the duckpond, the loaf of bread . . .

The time and motion study expert stopped to speak to the glamorous typist. 'I'm bound to tell you that I shall put in my report that you waste too much time on your appearance.' 'Go ahead,' she said, 'but I've only been here two months and I'm engaged to the boss, so it's not been entirely wasted.'

'What was Dick Turpin famous for?' 'He was one of the first road-users to cause a hold-up.'

'Beneath my husband's cold hard exterior – there's a cold, hard interior.'

Molly: What's the last thing you take off before going to bed?
Harold: My feet off the floor.

Bernie: Dad, would you do my arithmetic for me.
Dad: No, son, it wouldn't be right.
Bernie: Well, at least you could try.

Religious teacher: When was medicine first mentioned in the Bible?
Brian: When the Lord gave Moses two tablets.

Friend: I suppose being a dentist is very interesting.
Dentist: Not really – the drilling gets a bit boring.

Ted: What was it the hungry donkey said when he only had thistles to eat?
Ned: Thisle have to do.

Mr Briggs was making a knotty pine bookcase. His young son pointed to it and said, 'What are those holes for?'
'They're *knot* holes,' replied his father.
'Well,' said the lad, 'if they're not holes, what are they?'

Stewart: Mum, can I have five pence
for the old man who's crying
outside?
Mother: of course, dear, but what's
the old man crying about?
Stewart: He's crying 'Ice lollies,
fivepence each.'

Office Manager: How well can you
type?
Dolly: Oh not very well, but I can
rub out at sixty-five words a minute.

Physics teacher: Now on your
papers, I want you to write down
what you know about nuclear fission.
He was taken aback to read on
Jimmy Brown's paper 'Nothing.'

Ollie was looking at cars with a view
to buying one.
He pointed to a lovely streamlined
job: 'Is that a fast car?' he asked the
salesman. 'Fast,' said the salesman.
'If you got in that car now you'd be in
John o'Groats by two o'clock
tomorrow.'
Ollie went home to think about it but
came back next day. 'I've decided not
to buy it,' he said, 'I can't think of
any reason why I should be in John
o'Groats at two o'clock tomorrow.'

Tim at boarding school, sent this telegram to his father asking for money: 'No mon, no fun, your son.' Back came the reply, 'How sad, too bad, your dad.'

Smart Alec: What goes up a bell rope wrapped in greaseproof paper?
Clever Dick: The lunchpack of Notre Dame.

The office manager looked towards his secretary who was absorbed in painting her fingernails.
'Miss Bright,' he said, 'I'd like to compliment you on your work – but when are you going to do any?'

Polly: Why are you putting starch in your whisky?
Billy: Because I want a nice stiff drink.

A man in a train leaned forward and spoke to the man sitting opposite him.

'Do you realise,' he said, 'that you are reading your newspaper upside down?'

'Of course I realise it,' snapped the other. 'Do you think it's easy?'

After the telephone had been installed in her home, the lady called the operator.

'My telephone cord is too long,' she said. 'Would you please pull it a little from your end?'

Parents spend the first part of a child's life teaching him to walk and talk, and the rest of his childhood making him sit down and keep quiet.

Prison Officer: Sir, I have to report that ten prisoners have broken out.
Governor: Blow the whistles, sound the alarms, alert the police ...
Prison Officer: Shouldn't we call the doctor first – it looks as if it might be measles.

Andy: Why were the soldiers tired on April Fool's Day?
Sandy: Because they'd just had a March of thirty-one days.

When rooting round in the attic
Gordon found the old family Bible,
and when he opened it a large
pressed leaf fell out.
'Oh,' he said, 'Adam must have left
his clothes here.'

Maisie: Does a giraffe get a sore
throat if he gets his feet wet?
Daisy: I suppose so – but not until
the next week.

Goofy Gus had a rope hanging from
a tree outside his window.
'What's that for?' asked his brother.
It's my weather forecaster,' said
Gus. 'When it moves, it's windy, and
when it's wet, it's raining.'

Pete: Why do you always part your
hair in the middle?
Steve: So that I will be evenly
balanced when I ride my bicycle.

Lady customer: I'd like a shirt for my husband?
Assistant: Yes, madam, what size?
Lady customer: I don't know, but I can just get both my hands round his neck, if that's any help.

Jack: Did I ever tell you about the time I came face to face with a lion?
Joe: No, what happened?
Jack: Well, there I was without a gun. The lion growled menacingly, and crept closer and closer ....
Joe: Good heavens! What did you do?
Jack: I moved to the next cage.

Pam: You see, doctor, I'm always dizzy for half an hour after I get up in the morning.
Doctor: Well, try getting up half an hour later.

Little Bobby came home from school very fed up. 'I wish I'd lived in the olden days,' he said.
'Oh, why?' said his mother.
'Because then I wouldn't have so much history to learn.'

Worried lady passenger: Captain do ships this size sink very often?
Captain: No, madam, never more than once.

Mother was telling father what a naughty girl Debbie had been. She had had a fight with the boy opposite. 'It's all the fault of those dreadful Higgins children,' she said. 'She learned about biting and hair-pulling from them.'
'Yes,' said Debbie, 'but kicking on the shins was my own idea.'

A small boy was peering through a hole in a hedge of a Nature Camp. His friend came up to him and asked: 'Roger, what can you see? Are they men or women in there?'
'I can't tell,' replied Roger. 'None of them have any clothes on.'

Linda: Mummy, why do you have some grey hair?
Mummy: I expect it's because you are so naughty and cause me so much worry.
Linda: Oh – you must have been terrible to Grandma.

Auntie May: Well, Susan, what are you going to do when you're as big as your mother?
Susan: Go on a diet.

Clerk at Job Centre: Well they want somebody at the Eagle Laundry. Would you like to work there?
Young man: Well I've never washed any eagles, but I'm willing to give it a try.

Teacher: Sammy, what is water?
Sammy: Water is a colourless liquid that turns black when I put my hands in it.

In the snake-house at the zoo, one snake said to another:
'Are we supposed to be poisonous?'
'Why?'
'Well, I've just bitten my lip.'

Gilbert: My wife's a kleptomaniac.
Donald: Is she taking anything for it?

Fred: What was a tortoise doing on the M.1?
Bill: About two miles an hour.

Graham: Why is the nose in the middle of the face?
Mike: Because it's the centre.

Teacher: Which is more important, the sun or the moon?
Effie: The moon.
Teacher: Why do you think so?
Effie: Well the moon shines at night when it's dark, but the sun shines in the day when it's light anyway.

Mother: Terry did you fall down with your good trousers on?
Terry: Yes, mum, there wasn't time to take them off.

Brian: My wife has a marvellous mother – she's 82 and hasn't got one grey hair.
Bernie: Gosh, that's wonderful.
Brian: Yes – she's completely bald.

Doris: Why do they put telephone wires so high?
Morris: To keep up the conversation.

Father: How were your marks in the exam, son?
Son: Under water.
Father: What do you mean?
Son: Below C level.

Reggie: I shall buy a farm two miles long and a half inch wide.
Roger: What would you grow on a farm that size?
Reggie: Spaghetti.

Emmy: How do you make notes of stone?
Jamie: I don't know.
Emmy: Just rearrange the letters.

Norman: I understand your brother had an accident when he joined the submarine service?
Alan: Yes – he couldn't get out of the habit of opening the windows at night when he went to bed.

Clive: I saw you pushing your bicycle to work this morning.
Ben: Yes, I was so late I didn't have time to get on it.

Jed: Why did the pioneers cross to
the West in covered wagons?
Ned: I suppose they didn't want to
wait forty years for a train.

Two men sat next to each other in the
Doctor's waiting room.
'I'm aching from arthritis.' said one.
'I'm B. Bent from Birmingham,'
said the other. 'Glad to know you.'

Husband: You hadn't a rag on your
back when I married you.
Wife: Well, I've certainly got plenty
now.

Teacher: Desmond, this is the fifth
day this week you've had to stay
behind after school. What have you
to say for yourself?
Desmond: I'm certainly glad it's
Friday.

Tim: Is it legal for a man to marry his widow's sister?
Tom: Hardly – that man would be dead.

Phil: May I have a hot-dog?
Bill: With pleasure.
Phil: No – with sauce and pickles, please.

A soldier was walking along a country road with a pack on his back, and was offered a lift by a driver with an old dilapidated truck. The driver noticed the soldier was still carrying his pack on his back. 'Why don't you take that thing off your back?' said the driver. 'Well your truck seems so old, I thought I'd help by carrying this load myself.'

1st Cannibal: **Am I late for lunch?**
2nd Cannibal: **Yes, everybody's eaten.**

Emily: **Why is the sky so high?**
Lou: **So the birds won't bump their heads.**

Silly Billy: **I eat small pieces of metal every day.**
Friend: **Why do you do that?**
Silly Billy: **It's my staple diet.**

'My husband is so mean he complained to the doctor that he'd got better before his medicine was used up.'

Dickie: **I think girls are too biased.**
Rickie: **What do you mean?**
Dickie: **It's bias this and bias that – till we're broke.**

Dentist: **What sort of filling would you like in your tooth?**
Little Jemima: **Chocolate, please.**

Archie: **I'm glad I'm back from holiday – it rained all the time.**
Reggie: **It couldn't have been that bad; you've got a nice tan.**
Archie: **That's not tan, it's rust.**

'I'm afraid this food is all going to waist,' said the fat lady as she sat down to her dinner.

A Scotsman died and went to Heaven.
'Hi there,' he called. 'I'm Jock MacTavish and I've been sent to Heaven.'
'Go away,' called St Peter, 'I'm not going to make porridge just for one.'

Briggs: My uncle disappeared when he was on safari.
Bloggs: What happened to him?
Briggs: My dad says something he disagreed with ate him.

'If my husband ever had any get-up-and-go, it had got up and gone before I met him.'

Landlady (to young man who is seeking accommodation): I like to keep my house quiet – have you any children?
Young man: No.
Landlady: Any musical instruments, radio, cat or dog or other pet?
Young man: No – but my fountain pen scratches a little.

A man registered at a small hotel, and asked the manager, 'Are the sheets clean?'
'Of course they are,' said the manager. 'I washed them myself this morning – if you don't believe me you can feel them; they're still damp.'

Jack: My uncle swallowed a frog.
Jill: Goodness, did it make him sick?
Jack: Sick! He's liable to croak any minute.

A theatrical impresario was approached by a man who was bankrupt. 'I have a suggestion to put to you,' he said. 'Put £20,000 in the bank for my wife, 'he said, 'and I'll commit suicide on your stage ... all London will come to see it.'
'No thanks,' said the impresario. 'What could you do for an encore?'

Father: Where did your mother go?
Son: She's round at the front.
Father: I know what she looks like, I want to know where she is.

Dan: My kid brother thought a football coach had four wheels.
Stan: How many does it have?

Caller at door: Do you believe in the hereafter, madam?
Woman: Yes.
Caller: Well, I'm the landlord, and I'm hereafter the rent.

Beryl: What happened to the human cannon-ball at the circus?
Daryl: He got fired.

Garry: I went to see a psychiatrist about my poor memory.
Barry: What did he do?
Garry: He made me pay in advance.

Garry: (to his bride): Would you be very angry with me if I confess that my upper teeth are false?
Gloria: Of course not, darling. Now I can relax and take off my wig, my inflatable bra and my wooden leg.

Jessica: Is it correct to say that you water your horse?
Mother: Yes, dear.
Jessica: Then I'm going to milk my cat.

A little chap was walking home late at night, when he was attacked from behind. He fought like mad, but finally the thieves got him down and searched his pockets. All they found was ten pence.
'Why did you put up such a fight for tenpence?' one asked.
'I thought you were after the two hundred pounds in my shoe.'

Joe: When does a bed change size?
Jack: At night, when two feet are added to it.

Two Hippies walked into a restaurant but were stopped at the door. 'You can't come in here without a tie,' the doorman said.

'Okay man,' said one Hippie and left, returning a few minutes later wearing a tie.

The doorman turned to the other Hippie. 'What about him?' he said.

'Him?' said the Hippie, 'That's my wife!'

Steve: How did you get that black eye?

Stan: I got hit by a guided muscle.

Bus conductor: Come down – you can't stand on the top of this bus.

Goofy Gus: And why not?

Bus conductor: It's a single decker.

Mandy: Where does Friday come before Thursday?

Sandy: In a dictionary.

Nellie: I'm very glad I wasn't born in Spain.
Wallie: Why is that?
Nellie: I can't speak a word of Spanish.

Ambulance men (to boy injured on the road): Tell me your name, son so that I can notify your family.
Boy: My family already know my name.

Cecil: What is black and white and red all over?
Algy: A newspaper?
Cecil: No, a sunburnt zebra.

Teacher: What does HNO_3 stand for?
Smart Alec: Er .. let me see now … it's on the tip of my tongue.
Teacher: Well, you'd better spit it out quick – it's nitric acid.

Pamela visited the greengrocers with her mother, and the greengrocer gave her an apple.
'What do you say Pamela?' said her mother.
'Will you please peel it?' replied Pamela.

Clive: How old is your brother?
Steve: He's a year old.
Clive: Well I've got a dog who's a year old and he can walk twice as far as your brother.
Steve: He's got twice as many legs.

Customer: Waiter, I don't like all the flies in here.
Waiter: Well, just point out the ones you don't like and I'll have them put out.

Father: Who gave you that black eye?
Jack: Nobody – I had to fight for it.

Daisy: Do you know how to make a Maltese cross?
Maisie: Stick your finger in his eye.

194

Auntie: Come on, Billy dear, eat up your cabbage, it's good for growing children.
Billy: I don't want to grow any children.

Judge: You've been convicted six times of this offence. Aren't you ashamed of yourself?
Prisoner: No, your Honour. I don't think one should be ashamed of one's convictions.

Les: What can run across the floor but has no legs?
Des: Water.

Eric: Why can't a bicycle stand up by itself?
Derrick: Because it's two tyred.

Beryl: Why are contortionists thrifty people?
Cheryl: Because they can make both ends meets.

Briefing Officer (to new air hostess): What would you do if you found yourself in a shallow dive?
Air Hostess: I'd drink up quickly and get out.

Doctor: You need glasses.
Patient: How can you tell?
Doctor: I knew as soon as you came in the window.

Teacher: (to Parent on open day: Yes, Mr Brown, I think your son will go down in History ....
Mr Brown: Oh, really ...
Teacher: Yes, and in English, Maths and Science.

Rupert: How many dead people are there in a cemetery?
Robert: All of them.

Teacher: We all know that when certain substances are heated they expand, and when they are cooled they contract. Can anyone give me an example of this?
Freddie: Well, in the winter the days are short and in the summer the days are long.

Tilly: Why did the germ cross the microscope?
Billy: To get to the other slide.

Wally: If you were surrounded by twenty lions, fifteen tigers, and twelve leopards, how would you get away from them.
Sally: I'd wait for the merry-go-round to stop and get off!

An American was seen putting on his bathing trunks in the middle of a desert. An Arab rode past and said to him; You know, the sea is six hundred miles from here?'
'Six hundred miles,' said the American. 'Brother – some beach!'

Sherlock Holmes was visited by his friend Doctor Watson.
'Morning, Watson,' said the great detective – 'Isn't it a bit warm to be wearing your red flannel underwear?'
'How amazing, Holmes!' How on earth could you detect that I am wearing my red flannel underwear?'
'Elementary, my dear Watson. You've forgotten to put on your trousers.'

The old man at the cinema was grubbing round under the seat to the annoyance of the lady next to him.
'I've dropped my toffee,' he explained.
'Can't you leave it until the end?' she said crossly.
'No, it's got my false teeth stuck to it.'

Teacher: Can anybody tell me something about Christopher Columbus?
Desmond: He discovered America and was very economical.
Teacher: How do you mean, economical?
Desmond: He was the only man to travel thirty thousand miles on a galleon.

Mother: I've told you a million times not to exaggerate.

Sandra: Darling, will you love me still when my hair has gone all grey? *Donald:* Of course I will. If I loved you when your hair was blonde, then brunette then black then red – why should grey make any difference?

Noah (to his son Ham who is fishing): Go easy on the bait, remember I've only got two worms.

Angie: Why do storks lift only one leg? *Georgie:* If they lifted the other leg they'd fall over.

Wynn: Whenever I'm down in the dumps I buy new clothes. *Len:* So that's where you get them!

Briggs: What's worse than raining cats and dogs?
Bloggs: Hailing taxis.

Policeman: I'm afraid I'm going to lock you up for the night.
Hooligan: Why – what's the charge?
Policeman: Oh, there's no charge – it's all part of the service.

A spoilt child was making a nuisance of himself laying in the aisle of the aeroplane to the particular annoyance of one passenger who wanted to doze.
'I say, kid,' he said, 'why don't you go outside and play!'

Milly: What are you writing?
Molly: I'm writing a letter to myself.
Milly: What does it say?
Molly: How do I know – I won't get it till tomorrow.

Flora: How much money do you have on you?
Dora: Between £68 and £70.
Flora: Isn't that rather a lot to be carrying around?
Dora: No – Two pounds isn't very much.

Lady patient: I seem to get fat in certain places, Doctor, what should I do?

Doctor: Stay out of those places.

Dopey Dan: What's that iron box for?

Gormless Gus: That's my pillow.

Dopey Dan: Won't it be a bit hard?

Gormless Gus: Not when I've stuffed it with feathers.

Mother: You're mopping up the spilled coffee with cake?

Brenda: Well, it's sponge cake, isn't it?

Jimmy: Mum, can I go out and play?

Mother: What, with those holes in your trousers?

Jimmy: No, with the kids next door.

Diner: Waiter, this meat isn't fit for a pig.
Waiter: I'll take it back, sir, and bring you some that is.

Gertie: (shaking her husband): Bertie, I heard a mouse squeak.
Bertie: What do you want me to do – oil it?

Customer: Waiter, I asked for lentil soup – this tastes like soap.
Waiter: Oh, sorry sir – that must be tomato – the lentil tastes like petrol.

Freddie: I can't leave you.
Trudie: Do you love me so much?
Freddie: No, you're standing on my foot.

Cecil: How can one person make so many mistakes in a single day?
Basil: I get up early.

Hotel Manager: Well, sir did you enjoy your stay with us?
Guest: Yes, but it seems hard to leave the place so soon after buying it.

A woman walked into a smart dress shop in Bond Street and said to an assistant:
'Would you take that dress with the red flowers, and flowing scarf out of the window, please?'
'Certainly, madam, I'll do that right away,'
'Thank you,' said the woman, 'it annoys me every time I pass.'

Psychiatrists inform us that one out of four people are mentally ill. So check your friends – if three of them are all right – it must be you!

Mrs Griggs: My husband beats me up every morning.
Mrs Spriggs: How terrible!
Mrs Griggs: Yes, he gets up at seven and I get up at eight.

Doris: Now that we're engaged, I hope you'll give me a ring.
Horace: Of course, what's your number?

Policeman: Here – why are you trying to cross the road in this dangerous place? There's a zebra crossing just a few yards up the road.
Pedestrian: Well, I hope he's having better luck than I am.

Terry: Why is the Post Office not having to have telephone poles any longer?
Gerry: Because they're long enough.

Pat: How did you manage to crash your car?
Matt: You see that ditch over there?
Pat: Yes.
Matt: Well, I didn't.

Charlie: Why does it rain, dad?
Dad: To make the grass and the flowers grow.
Charlie: Well, why does it rain on the pavement?

Young Joey: My mother has the worst memory in the world?
Young Billy: Does she forget everything?
Young Joey: No – she remembers everything.

Tess: Jumping off Blackpool Tower isn't dangerous.
Jess: How on earth can you say that?
Tess: The jumping isn't dangerous – it's the sudden stop that is.

Charlie: Mum, Buster's broke a window.
Mother: How did he do that?
Charlie: I threw a stone at him and he ducked!

'Doctor, my hair keeps falling out. Can you recommend anything to keep it in?'
'How about a cardboard box!'

Husband: This coffee tastes awful.
Wife: I can't understand why. It's fresh – I made it in my dressing gown.
Husband: No wonder it tastes funny.

There was a knock on the door when a lady was taking her bath.
'Who's there?' she called.
'Blind man!'
Hearing this the lady said she'd be right there, and stepping out of the bath, she opened the door.
'Where do you want me to put these Venetian blinds, lady?' said the surprised man.

Ted: Did you say your dog's bark was worse than his bite?
Ned: Yes.
Ted: Then for heaven's sake, don't let him bark – he just bit me.

Teacher: How old were you on your last birthday?
Brian: Seven.
Teacher: And how old will you be on your next birthday?
Brian: Nine.
Teacher: That's impossible.
Brian: No it isn't, sir. I'm eight today.

Pilot: First one wing came off, then the other.
Young lady: Good heavens, what did you do?
Pilot: I grabbed a drumstick and had a second helping.

Percy: If you won't marry me, I'll hang myself in front of your house.
Marylyn: Please don't, you know father doesn't like to see you hanging around.

Father: The man who marries my daughter will get a prize.
Claud: Can I see the prize first?

Tramp: I haven't had more than one meal this week, lady.
Fat Lady: How I wish I had your willpower.

Mother: How do you like your new teacher?

Susie: Not very much.

Mother: Why is that?

Susie: She told me to sit in front for the present, but she didn't give me any present.

Teacher: Why are you late this morning, Sandra?

Sandra: Because of the sign down the road.

Teacher: What sign?

Sandra: It says 'Go Slow – School ahead'.

Wally: I'm having trouble with impetigo, miss.

Teacher: Good heavens, where do you have it?

Wally: I don't have it – I just can't spell it.

Teacher: If you had ten pence and you asked your father for another tenpence, how much would you have?

Archie: Ten pence.

Teacher: You don't know your arithmetic.

Archie: You don't know my father.

Andy: I'd like to marry a girl who could take a joke.

Sally: That's the only kind you'll get.

Keith: Don't you think I sing with feeling?
Maisie: No – if you had any feeling you wouldn't sing.

Ron: What does it mean when the barometer is falling?
Don: It means that whoever nailed it up didn't do a very good job.

Barney: Why didn't they bury the Duke of Wellington with full military honours in 1850?
Bernie: Because he didn't die until 1852.

Mickie: Why did Robinson Crusoe always have long week-ends?
Dickie: He got all his work done by Friday.

Dan: Have you ever hunted bear?
Sam: No, but I've been fishing in my shorts.

Duncan: Where does a seven foot gorilla sleep?
Duggie: Anywhere he wants to.

Commuter: What's the good of your timetable? The trains are never on time.
Porter: And how would you know they were late if it wasn't for the timetable?

Tramp: Would you give me 25 pence for a sandwich, lady?
Lady: I don't know – let me see the sandwich.

Customer: Waiter, why is this bath-bun all smashed up?
Waiter: You said you wanted a coffee and a bath-bun, and step on it, so I did.

Lindy: Can you skate?
Mandy: I don't know; I can't stand up long enough to find out.

Teacher: But I told you all to draw a ring, and you've drawn a square, Willy.
Willy: It's a boxing-ring, miss.

Bertram: How did you manage to pass the geometry test without doing any studying?
Smart Alec: Oh, I knew all the angles.

Tom: Will you lend me ten pounds?
Tim: I'm sorry, I can't spare ten pounds.
Tom: All right – lend me ten pounds and give me five pounds now. Then I'll owe you five pounds, and you'll owe me five pounds, and we'll call it square.

Chrissie, the kleptomaniac, was very grateful to her doctor for his helping in curing her affliction. 'How can I ever repay you, doctor?' she asked. 'Well, if you should have a remission,' he said, 'I could do with some binoculars.'

Clever Dick: How many peas are there in a pint?
Bozo: How many?
Clever Dick: One!

Two rich big-headed men met in a swanky hotel.
Said one: 'I'm thinking of buying all the gold-mines in the world.'
The other replied, 'I'm not sure I want to sell them.'

Visitor to Farm: Do you know how long cows should be milked?
Farmer: The same as short ones.

The bus was crowded and as one more man tried to get on the passengers wouldn't let him board.
'It's too crowded,' they said. 'Who do you think you are?'
'I'm the driver,' he said.

Teacher: John, give me an example
of a double negative.
John: I don't know none, miss.
Teacher: Correct.

Freda: My sister is black and blue
because she puts on cold cream, face
cream, wrinkle cream, vanishing
cream, hair cream, and skin cream
every night.
Rhoda: But why does that make her
black and blue?
Freda: She keeps on slipping out of
bed.

Gordon: What would you do if you
found £500,000.
Geoff: Well, if it was a poor person
who'd lost it, I'd return it.

Gracie: The trouble with you is
you're always wishing for something
you don't have.
Tracey: What else is there to wish
for?

'We're sending our little Willy to
camp for the summer.'
'Does he need a holiday?'
'No – we do.'

Polly: Mummy I got a hundred in school today.
Mummy: That's splendid, dear. What did you get a hundred for?
Polly: Two things. I got 50 in English, and 50 in arithmetic.

'My son is a true hippy – he'd sooner starve to death than eat a square meal.'

Tessie: This hot weather gets me down.
Bessie: Well, why don't you throw the thermometer out of the window and watch the temperature drop!

Buster: Oh, my new shoes hurt me something awful.
Teddy: No wonder, you've got them on the wrong feet.
Buster: But I haven't got any other feet.

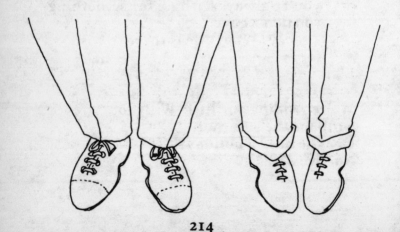

Willy: What does your mother do for a headache?
Jimmy: She sends me out to play.

An old couple in Wales out walking had lost their way, and darkness was falling. They spotted a man and a woman in a field tending their sheep, and asked them how far it was to the nearest town.
'Oh, five miles, isn't it,' said Ifan. Seeing the old couple's faces fall, Megan whispered, 'Make it two miles, Ifan, can't you see how tired they are.'

Sammy: There's a man at the door with a wooden leg called Owen.
Father: What's his other leg called?

Penny: What is always coming but never arrives?
Lenny: Tomorrow.

Newcomer: Bertie always wanted to be a stage magician and saw people in half.
Neighbour: Is he an only one?
Newcomer: Oh no, he has several half-brothers and sisters.

Archie: What are you doing?
Reggie: I've just painted a picture of a horse eating hay.
Archie: Where's the hay?
Reggie: The horse has eaten it.
Archie: Where's the horse?
Reggie: Well, it's gone – there's no point in him hanging about when all the hay's gone.

Chemistry teacher: Can anyone tell me a deadly poison?
Tommy: Aviation.
Chemistry teacher: Aviation?
Tommy: Yes – one drop and you're dead.

Learn from the mistakes of others – you can't live long enough to make them all by yourself.

Tina: Which members of an orchestra can't you trust?
Tony: The fiddlers.

Patient: You were right when you said you'd have me on my feet and walking in no time.
Doctor: That's good; when did you start walking?
Patient: When I got your bill – I had to sell my car to pay it.

Judge: The next man to raise his voice in this court will be thrown out.
Prisoner: HOORAY!

Briggs: Is your house warm?
Bloggs: It should be. I gave it three coats last week.

Coroner (to widow): Can you remember what your husband's last words were, madam?
Widow: Yes, he said, 'I don't see how they can make a profit selling this salmon at ten pence a tin.'

The girlfriend of a hold-up man visited him in prison.
'The money,' he whispered, 'is it safe?'
'Safe as the bank of England,' she assured him. 'They've built a 25-story block of flats on top of it.'

The trumpet-player had been blasting away all day, when there was a knock on his door.

'I live next door to you,' he explained. 'Do you know I work nights?'

'No', said the trumpet-player, 'but if you hum a few bars I'll get the melody.'

Mavis: Does your cat have fleas?
Toots: Don't be silly, cats don't have fleas, they have kittens.

Receptionist: Doctor, there's an invisible man here to consult you.
Doctor: Tell him I can't see him.

Effie: I've just swallowed a bone.
Mother: Are you choking?
Effie: No, I'm serious.

The lady said a polite 'Good-morning' to the Vicar as he passed.
'Mummy,' said Harry, 'who was that man?'
'That's the man who married me,' said Mother.
'In that case,' said Harry, 'who's that man hanging around our house that I call daddy?'

Ernie: How did you get that swelling on your nose?
Bernie: I bent down to smell a brose.
Ernie: There's no 'b' in rose.
Bernie: There was in this one.

Mrs Hobbs to neighbour: 'My husband always called a spade a spade until he tripped over one in the dark.'

The man coming round after being involved in an accident, found himself in hospital, and turned to the man in the next bed:
'Was I brought here to die?' he asked.
Cockney patient: 'No, you were brought here yesterdie.'

Willy: What makes you think your mother wants to get rid of you?
Wally: Why else would she pack my lunch every day in a road map?

Sidney: Show me a tough guy and I'll show you a coward.
Briggy: Well, I'm a tough guy.
Sidney: I'm a coward.

Neighbour: Your daughter is only four and can spell her name backwards? What's her name?
Proud Mother: Ada.

Molly: Have you heard the latest. It's all over the building.
Milly: What's all over the building?
Molly: The roof.

Monty: I can stay under water for ten minutes.
Tony: Impossible.
Monty got a tumbler of water and put it on his head.

Patient: Doctor, I'm very bothered
about my breathing, Doctor.
Doctor: Oh, we'll soon find
something to stop that.

Conceited pundit: Have you seen me
on television?
Acquaintance: Yes, on and off.
Pundit: And how did you like me?
Acquaintance: Off.

Eddie: If two's company and three's
a crowd, what are four and five?
Edie: Nine.

Buster: Why can't two elephants go
into a swimming pool at the same
time?
Lester: Because they have only one
pair of trunks.

The family had enjoyed their holiday on the farm and wrote again the following year to book a fortnight.

In his letter, Mr Brown wrote to the farmer 'The only thing we didn't enjoy was the noise the pigs made.' The farmer wrote back, 'Don't worry, sir, we haven't had any pigs here since you left.'

Roger: Oh, he's a friendly dog, he'll eat off your hand.
Lodger: That's what I'm afraid of.

Blondie: I'd like a knickerbocker glory, with double creams, raspberry syrup, chocolate chips, and lots of ice cream.
Waiter: Would you like a cherry on top?
Blondie: Oh no – I'm on a diet.

Des: Do you know why bears have fur coats?
Les: Well, they'd look a bit silly in plastic macs.

The Texan was showing Laird Macintosh round his vast ranch, and boasting that he had 4,000 head of cattle.
'Well, man,' said the Laird – 'I have 5,000 cattle in my lands in Scotland.'
The Texan quickly replied, 'What I meant, my lord, was that I have 4,000 head of cattle in the freezer.'

Shopper: What? 80 pence a pound for butter? Down the road it's only 60 pence.
Grocer: Well, why don't you go and get it there?
Shopper: Well, they're out of it.
Grocer: Well, when I'm out of it, mine's only 50 pence a pound.

Householder (to insurance salesman) Give me one good reason why I should purchase your insurance policy.
Insurance salesman: Well, last week I sold a policy to a man near here, and the following day he was trapped under a lorry, and we paid out £10,000. Just think, you might be just as lucky.

The helicopter had been on its mercy
mission combing the snowy wastes
of Scotland. The pilot spotted a curl
of smoke coming from a half-buried
chimney, and descended. He called
down through the chimney: 'Is there
anybody there?'
'Yes. Who are you?'
'We're the mountain rescue
helicopter and we're hovering over
your house.'
'Well, go away, we bought a flat off
you last year.'

Lecturer to Chairman: May I sit on
your right hand?
Chairman: You may – but I'll need it
later to ring the bell with.

MORE CRAZY JOKES

JANET ROGERS

illustrations by

ROBERT NIXON

999. *What do hot dogs have to do with outer space?*
They are UFOs – Unidentified Frying Objects!

998. *What makes a cemetery a very noisy place?*
The coffin.

997. FATHER TO SON: I don't care if the basement wall *is* cracking. Please stop telling everyone you come from a broken home.

996. MOTHER TO LITTLE BOY: *Do you know the difference between an elephant and a post box?*
LITTLE BOY: No.
MOTHER: *Well, I'd better not send you to post a letter!*

995. *How does Batman's mother call him for his lunch?*
Batman, din-ner, din-ner, din-ner, din-ner, d-i-n-n-e-r!

994. *Why did the little boy go to night school?*
So he could learn to read in the dark.

993. *'Nurse, I'm at death's door.'*
'Don't worry – the doctor will pull you through.'

992. *Why did the house want to see a doctor?*
Because it had window panes!

991. Did you hear about the thief who robbed a music shop and ran off with the lute?

990. *Notice in a wig-maker's shop window:*
If your hair isn't becoming to you,
it should be coming to us!

989. *'Have you any dogs going cheap?'*
'No, Sir. All our dogs go woof.'

988. *What's grey with a big trunk?*
A mouse going on holiday!

987. *What goes 99-plonk, 99-plonk?*
A centipede with a wooden leg.

986. *What time did the Chinese man go to the dentist?*
Tooth-hurty!

985. *Why don't elephants eat penguins?*
They can't get the wrappers off.

984. *Where does an orang-outang sleep?*
Anywhere it wants to.

983. *What did Tarzan say when he saw a herd of elephants
coming towards him?*
'Here come the elephants.'
Why do elephants wear dark glasses?
So they won't be recognised.
*What did Tarzan say when he saw a herd of elephants
coming towards him wearing dark glasses?*
Nothing, he didn't recognise them.

982. *Why did your cat join the Red Cross?*
It wants to be a first aid kit.

981. *Why does a cow wear a bell?*
Its horns don't work.

980. CANNIBAL CHIEF (*to his daughter*): It's high time you
got married. We'd better start looking for an edible
bachelor.

979. *What did one Hawaiian say to the other Hawaiian when they hadn't seen each other for a long time?*
'Ha – wa – ya.'

978. *Can an elephant jump higher than a lamp-post?*
Yes. Lamp-posts can't jump.

977. *Why did the monster go to hospital?*
To have his ghoul stones removed.

976. *When is a door not a door?*
When it's ajar!

975. *What do you get if you cross a hedgehog with a giraffe?*
A ten-foot toothbrush.

974. *What is a phantomime?*
A play acted by ghosts.

973. TEACHER TO LITTLE GIRL: *Is that a letter to your friend? You're writing it very slowly.*
LITTLE GIRL: I know. My friend can't read very fast.

972. *How do you make a waterfall?*
Throw a bucket of water out of the window.

971. *Knock, knock.*
Who's there?
Teresa.
Teresa who?
Teresa Green.

970. *How does a witch travel?*
By witchcraft.

969. *What is wet, black, floats on water and shouts 'knickers'?*
Crude oil.

968. *What do you call a bald rabbit?*
Hareless.

967. *What's yellow and zooms through the jungle at 100 mph?*
An E-type banana.

966. *What is a signature?*
A baby swan's autograph.

965. *Why did the hot dog climb to the top of the roof?*
He heard that the meal was on the house.

964.   *Why does Big Ears wear brown boots?*
       Because his black ones are at the menders.

963.   *'Operator, Operator, I must speak to the king of the
          jungle.'*
       'I'm sorry, Sir, but the lion is busy.'

962.   *A team of monsters playing football – who stands in
          goal?*
       The Ghoulie, of course.

961.   *What's big, red, and lies upside down in the gutter?*
       A dead bus.

960.   Mary had a parrot,
          She killed it in a rage,
       For every time her boyfriend came,
       The darn thing told her age.

959.   Sign in restaurant window:
       EAT NOW – PAY WAITER.

958.   *Where do baby monsters come from?*
       Frankenstorks.

957.   Did you hear about the man who shot his clock?
       He felt like killing time.

956.   *What is wet, soft and sings, 'When I'm cleaning
          windows'?*
       Chamois Davis Jr.

955.   *What is black, white and red all over?*
       A sunburned zebra.

954. *'Doctor, Doctor, I keep seeing spotted zebras.'*
'Have you ever seen a psychiatrist?'
'No, I've only seen spotted zebras.'

953. *How many wives is a man given in the marriage service?*
Sixteen – four better, four worse, four richer, four poorer.

952. *What is big and green and has a trunk?*
An unripe elephant.

951. *What do geese eat?*
Gooseberries.

950. ONE CANNIBAL TO ANOTHER: *Am I late for supper?*
SECOND CANNIBAL: Yes, everyone's already eaten.

949. Did you hear about the boy who wore a wet shirt all day? The label on the back said 'wash and wear'.

948. *Why did you leave your job?*
Illness.
Nothing serious, I hope?
Well, sort of; the boss got sick of me.

947. SNOOTY LADY: *I'm going to enter Fifi in the dog show next month.*
FRIEND: Ooh, do you think she'll win any prizes?
SNOOTY LADY: *No, but she'll meet a nice class of dog.*

946. CHILD: *Mummy, Mummy, there's a man at the door with a bill.*
MOTHER: Don't be silly, dear, it's a duck with a hat on.

945. **FIRST LITTLE GIRL:** *Which is more correct: 'The yolk of an egg* is *white', or 'The yolk of an egg* are *white'?*
SECOND LITTLE GIRL: 'The yolk of an egg *is* white.'
FIRST LITTLE GIRL: *Don't be silly, it's yellow.*

944. *What is the definition of noise?*
A skeleton dancing on a tin roof.

943. *What is the definition of politics?*
A parrot that has swallowed a watch.

942. **SUE:** *Ouch, that water was hot.*
SALLY: You should have felt it before putting your hand in.

941. *Why can't a bike stand up by itself?*
Because it is two-tyred.

940. Did you hear about the man in hospital who took a turn for the nurse?

939. *Why is the figure 9 like a peacock?*
Because without a tail it is nothing.

938. **JOE:** *Is that dog of yours a watchdog?*
JACK: Yes.
JOE: *Can he tell me the time?*

937. *Why did the windowpane blush?*
Because it saw the weather-strip.

936. *What part of a car is the laziest?*
The wheels, they are always tyred.

935. Did you hear about the poor little fish that went deaf?
      All his friends clubbed together and bought him a
      herring aid.

934. *Who was the straightest man in the Bible?*
      Joseph, because King Pharaoh made a ruler out of
      him.

933. TOM: *What colours would you paint the sun and the
      wind?*
      TIM: The sun rose, and the wind blue.

932. FIRST MAN: *Every day my dog and I go for a tramp in
      the woods.*
      SECOND MAN: I bet your dog enjoys that.
      FIRST MAN: *He does, but the tramp's getting a bit fed
      up with it.*

931. Did you hear about the woman whose son was away in the army? He wrote and told her that he had grown another foot, so she knitted him another sock.

930. FIRST MAN: *I wonder how long a person can live without a brain?*
SECOND MAN: How old are you?

929. NURSE: *Doctor, there is an invisible man in the waiting room.*
DOCTOR: Tell him I can't see him.

928. FRED: *I don't believe it! There's a dog in the High Street handing out parking tickets.*
TED: Is it brown, with pointed ears and a long tail?
FRED: *Yes.*
TED: Well, no wonder. That's the town police dog!

927. *When is a well-dressed lion like a weed?*
When he's a dandelion (dandy lion).

926. *When is a vet busiest?*
When it rains cats and dogs.

925. *Where do policemen live?*
999 Letsbe Avenue.

924. *'What do you mean, your school is well thought of by everyone?'*
'Well, it's approved.'

923. Did you hear about the hedgehog who courted a scrubbing brush?

922. *The doctor stood by the bedside of the very sick patient and said: 'I cannot hide the fact that you are a very ill man. Is there anyone you would like to see?'*

'Yes,' replied the patient faintly. 'Another doctor.'

921. *Knock, knock.*
Who's there?
Iowa.
Iowa who?
Iowa lot of money to the income tax people.

920. Do you want to come to an Adam and Eve party? Leaves off at eleven.

919. *What do you get if you cross an alley cat with a canary?*
A peeping tom.

918. *When a girl slips on the ice, why can't her brother help her up?*
He can't be a brother and assist her (a sister) too.

917. *What is Italian, 182 ft high and absolutely scrumptious?*
The leaning tower of Pizza.

916. *What is a myth?*
A lady moth who hasn't got married.

915. MARY: *What is your worst fault?*
MONA: My vanity. I sit in front of the mirror for hours admiring my beauty.
MARY: *That's not vanity, dear. That's just a vivid imagination.*

15

914. Two rather anxious parents enquired after their son's first sex lesson at school that day. 'Oh,' said the boy, 'it was useless – we only had the theory today.'

913. FIRST PARENT: *What's your son going to be when he passes all his exams?*
SECOND PARENT: A pensioner.

912. ELEPHANT: *Why are you so weak and tiny?*
MOUSE: Well, I haven't been very well.

911. *What do monsters do every night at 10.30?*
Take a coffin break.

910. FARMER: *This is a dogwood tree.*
CITY MAN: How can you tell?
FARMER: *By its bark.*

909. Did you hear about the man who sat down at dusk and waited to see where the sun went? It finally dawned on him.

908. FATHER: *Well, son, how are your marks at school?*
SON: They're under water.
FATHER: *What do you mean?*
SON: Below 'C' level.

907. *What do we call a cat who has swallowed a duck?*
A 'duck-filled fatty puss'.

906. *What game do miners play in the pit?*
Mineopoly.

905. *What always walks with its head down?*
A nail in your shoe.

904. *Why did the man wear a lifejacket at night?*
Because he was sleeping on a water-bed.

903. *Knock, knock,*
Who's there?
Cantaloupe.
Cantaloupe who?
We cantaloupe tonight. My father's watching.

902. *What means of transportation gives people colds?*
A choo-choo train.

901. *What kind of job is it easy to stick to?*
Working in a glue factory.

900. *A shepherd had twelve sheep. All but nine died. How many did he have left?*
Nine.

899. *What do you use to treat a pig with a sore throat?*
Oinkment.

898. JACK: *Did anyone laugh when you fell on the ice?*
JILL: No, but the ice made some terrible cracks.

897. *What did Napoleon become after his thirty-ninth year?*
Forty years old.

896. FATHER GHOST TO SON: Spook only when you are spoken to.

895. *Knock, knock.*
Who's there?
Isabel.
Isabel who?
Isabel ringing? I thought I heard one.

894. *Why does a golfer wear two pairs of trousers?*
In case he gets a hole-in-one.

893. *What is another name for a butcher's boy?*
A chop assistant.

892. *Who invented the first pen?*
The Incas (Inkers).

891. *Why did the elephant lie in the middle of the pathway?*
To trip up the ants.

890. *What is the difference between an elephant and peanut butter?*
The elephant doesn't stick to the roof of your mouth.

889. *What do you call a space magician?*
A flying saucerer.

888. *Are you mad if you talk to yourself?*
Not unless you answer.

887. It has recently been reported that Wales is sinking into the sea – due to the many leeks in the ground.

886. *What did the burglar say to the watchmaker?*
'So sorry to have taken so much of your valuable time.'

885. *What is a representative of the Waiters' Union called?*
A chop steward.

884. OFFICER: *Did you know your wife fell out of the car four miles back?*
MAN: Thank goodness for that – I thought I'd gone deaf!

883. *What would you get if you crossed a pig with Buzby?*
Crackling on the line.

882. *What do you call a flying policeman?*
A heli-copper.

881. *What kind of hat has fingerprints on it?*
A felt hat.

880. 'My doctor put me on a seafood diet.'
'Oh, really?'
'Yes, the more I see, the more I eat.'

879. *Who did the vampire marry?*
The girl necks door.

878. *Knock, knock.*
Who's there?
Amos.
Amos who?
Amosquito bit me! Ouch!

877.   PATIENT: *May I lie down on the floor instead of the couch?*
PSYCHIATRIST: Of course. Why?
PATIENT: *I want to discuss why my wife treats me like a doormat.*

876.   *What animal has two humps and is found at the North Pole?*
A lost camel.

875.   *What has four wheels and flies?*
A dustcart.

874.   *What is big, purple and lies in the sea?*
Grape Britain.

873.   When the weather is very bad and it's pouring with rain, owls aren't too keen to go courting. They just sit in the trees calling: 'Too wet to woo; too wet to woo.'

872.   *Who was one of the strongest dictators?*
Muscle-ini.

871.   'Who was that on the phone?' asked the wife.
'It was a wrong number, dear. Some chap looking for the Met. Office . . . wanted to know if the coast was clear.'

870.   JUDGE: *Haven't I seen you before?*
TAILOR: Maybe. So many people owe me money I don't remember all their faces.

869.   '*Why don't you have an automatic dishwasher?*'
'We don't have automatic dishes.'

868. *Why don't scarecrows have any fun?*
Because they are stuffed shirts.

867. *How do undertakers speak?*
Gravely.

866. *What kind of cattle laugh?*
Laughing stock.

865. MAN: *My sister married an Irishman.*
FRIEND: Oh, really.
MAN: *No, O'Reilly.*

864. *'How long have you been learning to skate?'*
'Oh, about a dozen sittings.'

863. Inscription on the tombstone of a hypochondriac:
'See – I *told* you I was ill.'

862. *'I hear your first two wives died of mushroom
poisoning. And now you say your third wife has
just died as a result of falling off a cliff. That's a bit
odd, isn't it?'*
'Not really. She wouldn't eat the poisoned
mushrooms.'

861. *What happens when you cross a police constable with
a ghost?*
You get an inspectre.

860. *What do short-sighted ghosts wear?*
Spooktacles.

859. Did you hear about the little boy who thought that his
Manx cat had lost its tail, so he took it to a retail
store to see if he could get a new one?

858. *What does an astronaut do when he gets angry?*
He blasts off.

857. *What monster has the best hearing?*
The eeriest, of course.

856. Did you hear about the man who went into an Irish
fish and chip shop? He said, 'Cod and chips, twice.'
'I heard you the first time,' said the man behind the
counter.

855. *What is the definition of double yellow lines in the
road?*
No parking at all; at all.

854. TEACHER: *Give me a sentence with the word
'centimetre' in it.*
GLADYS: My aunty was coming home from her
holidays and I was centimetre.

853. My husband believes so completely in reincarnation
that in his will he's left everything to himself.

852. *What is the difference between an engine driver and
a teacher?*
One minds the train, the other trains the mind.

851. *Can you spell 'Indian tent' with just two letters?*
TP.

850. *My wife's gone on holiday abroad.*
Jamaica?
No, she went of her own free will.

849. *Waiter, do you serve crabs?*
Sit down, Sir. We serve anybody.

848. *Where does a General keep his armies?*
Up his sleevies.

847. *How did you get to the hospital?*
Flu!

846. My wife has a better sense of judgement than I have: she chose me as her husband.

845. PUPIL: *Would you punish a pupil for something she didn't do?*
TEACHER: Of course not.
PUPIL: *Good, because I haven't done my homework.*

844. *What kind of a tie does a pig wear?*
A pigsty (pig's tie).

843. *Why do people feel stronger on Sundays?*
Because all the other days are week days (weak days).

842. BOSS: I don't like 'yes' men. When I say 'no' I want them to say 'no' too.

841. 'My wife says I'm effeminate. Compared to her, I suppose I am.'

840. *Why is music like an icy pavement?*
Because you will B flat if you don't C sharp.

839. *What is a person called who doesn't like Italian food?*
Antipasta!

838. *What is it that holds water yet is full of holes?*
A sponge.

837. **BARBER:** *I see your hair is beginning to abdicate at the top.*
CUSTOMER: Abdicate?
BARBER: *Yes, Sir. It's giving up the crown.*

836. Did you hear about the man who thought the Rover 3500 was a bionic dog?

835. *Why did Dracula leave Philadelphia in a hurry?*
Because it was a one-hearse town.

834. *Why did the elephant wear pink tennis shoes?*
Because he wanted to hide in the cherry tree.

833. *What happens if you cross a porcupine with a mole?*
You get a tunnel that leaks!

832. *Why is a large coat like a banana skin?*
Because they are both easy to slip on.

831. *Where does an American cow come from?*
Moo York.

830. *What animal eats the least?*
The moth. It just eats holes.

829. *Why do skeletons drink a lot of milk?*
Because it's good for the bones.

828. FIRST VAMPIRE: *How's business?*
SECOND VAMPIRE: Terrible. I had a letter today from my manager, saying I'm overdrawn fifty pints at the blood bank.

827. *When your clock strikes thirteen, what time is it?*
Time to get it fixed.

826. GEORGE: *Why does your dog go round and round in circles before it lies down?*
HENRY: Because he's a watchdog and he has to wind himself up.

825. *What is the best way to catch fish?*
Have someone throw them to you.

824. *What turned the moon pale?*
At-mos-fear.

823. *Who won the Monster Beauty Contest?*
Nobody.

822. *What yard has four feet?*
A back yard with a dog in it.

821.   *Why will 1984 be a good year for kangaroos?*
       Because it will be a leap year.

820.   YOUNG PRIEST: *He's confessed to stealing a crate of
           whisky. What shall I tell him?*
       OLD PRIEST: We don't pay more than £1 a bottle.

819.   *What did the wolf-man say when he saw Santa Claus?*
       'Yum, yum.'

818.   WIFE: *Did you know most accidents happen in the
           kitchen?*
       HUSBAND: I know – I have to eat them.

817.   *What particular dance do cleaners do?*
       The char-char.

816.   A tribe of cannibals were converted by missionaries
           to become good Catholics – they ate fishermen
           only on Fridays.

815.   BOSS: *Why are you late again this morning?*
       TYPIST: I'm afraid I overslept.
       BOSS: *You mean you sleep at home as well?*

814.   A German could not get his clock to work properly:
           no matter what he did with it, it would only *tick*.
           Finally, completely exasperated, the German held
           the clock firmly and said: 'Ve haf ways of making
           you tock.'

813.   *What is a vampire's favourite fruit?*
       A blood orange.

812.   FIRST IRISHMAN: *I'm Malone.*
       SECOND IRISHMAN: Sure, tis aisy to see you're by
          yourself since nobody is wid yer.

811.   ENGLISH TEACHER: *I am going to give you a sentence
          which I want you to correct: 'It was me that broke
          the window.'*
       PUPIL: It wasn't me that broke the window.

810.   *Where do fish wash themselves?*
       In the river basin.

809.   *Knock, knock,*
       Who's there?
       Sarah.
       Sarah who?
       Sarah doctor in the house?

808.   *Where did Noah keep his bees?*
       In ark hives.

807.   Hear about the two rabbits who got married and went
          on a bunnymoon?

806.   *Why was Adam a famous runner?*
       Because he was first in the human race.

805.   FIRST NUTCASE: *I find that time hangs heavily on
          my hands these days.*
       SECOND NUTCASE: Then why don't you get a
          wristwatch instead of that grandfather clock you're
          wearing?

804.   *What was King Alfred called after he had burnt the
          cake?*
       Alfred the Grate!

803. *What does a cat rest its head on when it goes to sleep?*
A caterpillar.

802. *Could you kill somebody just by throwing eggs at him?*
Yes, he would be eggs-terminated.

801. *How long did Cain hate his brother?*
As long as he was Abel.

800. *Why do women want husbands called William?*
So they can have a Will of their own.

799. JOHN: *What's the difference between lightning and electricity?*
JILL: I don't know.
JOHN: *Did you ever get a lightning bill?*

798. *Knock knock.*
Who's there?
Little old lady.
Little old lady who?
I didn't know you could yodel.

797. *Where were English kings usually crowned?*
On the head.

796. *Where do you find baby soldiers?*
In the infantry.

795. *Should you eat hamburgers on an empty stomach?*
No, you should eat them on a plate!

794. My dog is a terrible bloodhound. I cut my hand once
and he fainted.

793. *How do you make gold soup?*
Put 14 carrots in it.

792. *Why is the letter B hot?*
Because it makes oil boil.

791. *Have you seen the Duchess?*
No, but I have seen an English 'S'.

790. *What can fly underwater?*
A fly in a submarine.

789. The wonderful Wizard of Oz
Retired from business becoz
What with up-to-date science,
To most of his clients
He wasn't the wiz that he woz.

788. *Who has large antlers and wears white gloves?*
Mickey Moose.

787. *When are eyes not eyes?*
When the wind makes them water.

786. JOHNNY: *Mum, can I have the wishbone?*
MUM: Not till you've eaten your greens.
JOHNNY: *But Mum, I want to wish I won't have to eat them.*

785. GAME WARDEN: *You can't catch fish without a permit.*
FISHERMAN: I'm doing quite well with just worms, thank you.

784. *What kind of cake would most little boys not mind going without?*
A cake of soap.

783. *Are you going to take a bath?*
No – I'm going to leave it where it is.

782. *What part of a clock is always old?*
The second hand.

781. *Why did the dog howl?*
Because he barked up the wrong tree.

780. DOCTOR: *And how do you feel today, Mr Smith?*
MR SMITH: Same as usual, Doctor, with my hands.

779. 'Waiter, please get that fly out of my soup. I want to dine alone.'

778. TEACHER: *Sally, can you give me two pronouns?*
SALLY: Who, me?
TEACHER: *Correct.*

777. *Why does a chicken lay an egg?*
Because if she dropped it, it would break.

776. *When is a black dog not a black dog?*
When it is a greyhound.

775. MOTHER: *I've made the chicken soup.*
KIDS: Thank goodness for that. We thought it was for us.

774. FIRST MAN: *Where are you going to in such a hurry?*
SECOND MAN: To the doctor's – I don't like the look of my wife.
FIRST MAN: *Oh, can I come with you? I hate the sight of mine.*

773. *Where do all good turkeys go when they die?*
To oven.

772. *What's the best way to prevent infection from biting insects?*
Don't bite any.

771. *What is black and shiny and lives in trees and is highly dangerous?*
A crow with a submachine gun.

770. *Knock, knock.*
Who's there?
Tuba.
Tuba who?
Tuba toothpaste, please.

32

769. *Did you know Davy Crockett had three ears?*
No, how was that?
He had a right ear, a left ear, and a wild frontier.

768. *What coat has the most sleeves?*
A coat of arms.

767. *What do you do with sick kangaroos?*
Give them an Hoperation.

766. *If an apple a day keeps a doctor away, what will an onion do?*
Keep everyone away.

765. *Why is a fish shop always crowded?*
Because the fish fillet.

764. *Knock, knock.*
Who's there?
Iris.
Iris who?
Iris you were here.

763. *How can you tell there is an elephant in your sandwich?*
When it is too heavy to lift.

762. *Which three letters of the alphabet do all the work?*
N – R– G.

761. CUSTOMER: *Have you got some asparagus?*
WAITER: No, we don't serve sparrows and my name is *not* Gus.

760. My young son took his nose apart this morning – he wanted to see what made it run.

759. MOTHER: *When the new baby comes, do you want a baby brother or a baby sister?*
LITTLE BOY: I'd rather have a jelly baby.

758. *What is a stupid ant?*
An ignorant.

757. Did you hear about the two boa constrictors who got married? They had a crush on each other!

756. *What cups can't be drunk out of?*
Buttercups and hiccups.

34

755. *Did you enjoy your first day at school?*
Yes, but I've got to go back tomorrow.

754. *Why are policemen strong?*
Because they can hold up traffic.

753. *What's another name for a smart duck?*
A wise quacker.

752. BARBER: *How would you like your hair cut, sir?*
CUSTOMER: Off.

751. *When can you be said to have four hands?*
When you double your fists.

750. *What does a monster do when he loses his head?*
Calls for a head hunter.

749. TEACHER: *In what part of the world are people most ignorant?*
JACK: In London.
TEACHER: *Nonsense, why do you say that?*
JACK: Because my geography books says that's where the population is most dense.

748. *Knock, knock.*
Who's there?
Shirley.
Shirley who?
Shirley you must know me by now?

747. *Why did the boy give cough syrup to his pony?*
Someone had told him it was a little horse.

35

746. *What's red and swims in the ocean?*
Moby Bus.

745. *What happens to a cow when it stands out in the rain?*
It gets wet.

744. SISTER TO BROTHER: *How did Mum know you didn't have a bath?*
BROTHER: I forgot to wet the soap.

743. CUSTOMER: *I say, Mr Ironmonger, have you got 25-millimetre nails?*
IRONMONGER: Yes, Sir.
CUSTOMER: *Then scratch my back, will you? It's itching something terrible.*

742. *What do you call a budgie run over by a lawn mower?*
Shredded tweet.

741. *What game do ghosts play?*
Haunt and seek.

740. *Which dog is the most expensive?*
A deerhound (dear hound).

739. *What will the first clock on the moon be called?*
A luna-tick.

738. *What did the idiot call his pet tiger?*
Spot.

737. *What's yellow and black with red spots?*
A leopard with measles.

736. *Why did the girl put her bed in the fireplace?*
She wanted to sleep like a log.

735. *What is a sick reptile?*
An illigator.

734. My cellar is so damp that when I put down a mouse-trap, I catch fish.

733. A caterpillar is a worm with a sweater on.

732. My secretary is a miracle worker – it's a miracle if she works.

731. *'That's a strange pair of socks you've got on – one red and one yellow.'*
'I know – I've got another pair like that at home.'

730. *What do you call Eskimo cows?*
Eskimoos.

729. BILLY: *Mum thinks Dad's a real smasher.*
JOHN: That's nice of her.
BILLY: *Yes, that's why she never lets him do the washing up.*

728. *Where had the runner bean?*
To see the celery stalk.

727. *What moves around a bus at 1000 mph?*
A lightning conductor.

726. *What do lions sing at Christmas?*
Jungle bells, jungle bells.

725. *How can you keep a noisy dog quiet?*
With hush-puppies.

724. *How long does a candle burn?*
Oh, about one wick.

723. *Does your watch tell the time?*
No, I have to look at it.

722. *Knock, knock.*
Who's there?
Ida.
Ida who?
Ida baked a cake if Ida known you were coming.

721. I was teacher's pet. She couldn't afford a dog.

720. *When does it rain money?*
Whenever there's a change in the weather.

719. *What's better than a talking dog?*
A spelling bee.

718. *Why did all the opticians go to the Royal Tournament?*
Because it was a spectacle.

717. Did you hear about the boy who thought he was a magician? He went around the corner and turned into a sweet shop.

716. *Why doesn't a vampire spend much money on food?*
Because he eats necks to nothing.

715. *Knock, knock.*
Who's there?
Romeo.
Romeo who?
Romeover to the other side of the lake, and I'll tell you.

714. *Why don't bananas ever get lonely?*
Because they go around in bunches.

713. *How do you make a water-bed more comfortable?*
Use a water softener.

712. *What was the name of the first mechanical man to be invented?*
Frank N. Stein.

711. *'Tell me, do you have trouble making up your mind?'*
'Well, yes and no, Doctor.'

710. 'Is this a second-hand shop?'
'Yes.'
'Could you please fit one on my alarm clock then?'

709. What's the longest word in the dictionary?
Elastic. Because it stretches.

708. What's yellow and goes slam, slam, slam, slam?
A four-door banana.

707. FATHER: I found a horseshoe today. Do you know what that means?
SON: Perhaps the horse is walking in his stockinged feet!

706. Who makes up jokes about knitting?
A nitwit.

705. CUSTOMER: Do you have frog's legs?
WAITER: Yes, Sir.
CUSTOMER: Then hop into the kitchen and get me a sandwich.

704. What do you call a camel with three humps?
Humphrey.

703. Did you hear about the loony who buried his car battery because the mechanic told him it was dead.

702. Take away my first letter, then my second, then my third, fourth and fifth letters, and I remain the same. What am I?
A postman.

701. What kind of spy hangs around department stores?
A counterspy.

700. *What happens when you put snakes on a motor car window?*
You get windscreen vipers.

699. *Who has a parrot which shouts, 'Pieces of four! Pieces of four!'?*
Short John Silver.

698. *Knock, knock.*
Who's there?
Dwayne.
Dwayne who?
Dwayne the bath-tub, I'm dwowning.

697. *Why is the letter 'A' like a flower?*
Because a 'B' comes after it.

696. *What tree is hairy?*
A fur tree.

695. The local yokel sat dangling a fishing line down a manhole. The new parson gave him 50p and asked him kindly, 'How many have you caught today?'
'You be the tenth,' replied the yokel.

694. *What did the mother bee say to the baby bee?*
'Don't be naughty, honey, just beehive yourself while I comb your hair.'

693. *What happens to tyres when they get old?*
They are retired.

692. *What helps to keep your teeth together?*
Toothpaste.

691.   I eat my peas with honey,
       I've done it all my life,
       It may seem kind of funny,
       But it keeps them on my knife.

690.   *What is the difference between a fish and a piano?*
       You can't tuna fish.

689.   *Why did the simpleton put a chicken in a tub of hot
          water?*
       So she'd lay hard-boiled eggs.

688.   *Which king was entirely covered with thick hair?*
       King Kong.

687. *What's the cheapest way to post somebody?*
      Stamp on their foot.

686. 'I told you not to swallow!' yelled the dentist. 'That
      was my last pair of pliers.'

685. *'If frozen water is iced water, what is frozen ink?'*
      'Iced ink.'
      'You sure do.'

684. LITTLE BOY: *Show me a tough guy and I'll show you a
      coward.*
      BIG BOY: I'm a tough guy.
      LITTLE BOY: *Well, I'm a coward.*

683. My husband is so stupid he even takes a saddle to bed
      with him in case he has nightmares.

682. You know my rustproof, elephant-proof, shockproof,
      waterproof watch? Well, it's just caught fire.

681. *Why does an elephant wear plimsolls?*
      So he can sneak up on mice.

680. *Where do you take a sick horse?*
      To a horsepital.

679. *What is big, grey and mutters?*
      A mumbo jumbo.

678. *What did the jack say to the car?*
      'Can I give you a lift?'

677. *How can you tell an elephant from a monster?*
      A monster never remembers.

676. *Why did Mickey Mouse go on a journey to outer space?*
Because he wanted to find Pluto.

675. *How do you fit five elephants into a Mini?*
Two in the front, two in the back and one in the glove compartment.

674. *What rides on a motorcycle and eats cotton?*
Evil Boll Weevil.

673. *Knock, knock.*
Who's there?
Juno.
Juno who?
Juno what time it is?

672. FRED: *Mum, I don't like this cheese with holes in it.*
MUM: Stop being fussy. Eat the cheese and leave the holes at the side of your plate.

671. *How many people work in this office?*
Only about half of them.

670. *What do you get from nervous cows?*
Milk shakes.

669. *What do you call musical insects?*
Humbugs.

668. *What did they call prehistoric ship disasters?*
Tyrannosaurus wrecks.

667. 'My wife isn't pretty and she isn't ugly; she's pretty ugly.'

666. *Which car do hot dogs prefer to drive?*
A Rolls, of course.

665. *Knock, knock.*
Who's there?
Cargo.
Cargo who?
Cargo 'Beep, Beep.'

664. *When is a green book not a green book?*
When it is read.

663. *'Waiter, this plate is damp.'*
'I know, Sir, that's the soup.'

662. *How does an intruder get into the house?*
Intruder window.

661. *What do you call high-rise flats for pigs?*
Sty scrapers.

660. *Which fish go to heaven when they die?*
Angel fish.

659. *What sort of gun does a police dog use?*
A dogmatic.

658. *What would you see from the Eiffel Tower?*
Quite an eyeful.

657. Here lies a boy who played the fool,
When coming home one day from school,
He forgot his highway code,
What happened next, he never
    knowed.

656. **POLICEMAN TO MOTORIST:** *This is a one-way street.*
MOTORIST: Well I'm only going one way.

655. *What kind of ship was Dracula the captain of?*
A blood vessel.

654. *What do Eskimos call their money?*
Iced lolly.

653. Did you hear about the karate expert who joined the
army? The first time he saluted he nearly killed
himself.

652. *What is a hedgehog's favourite food?*
Prickled onions.

651. *What did the policeman say to his stomach?*
I've got you under a vest.

650. *What is a press photographer?*
A flash guy.

649. *How can you get into a locked cemetery at night?*
Use a skeleton key.

648. *Why was Batman sad in the autumn?*
Because Robin flew south.

647. *Which travels more slowly – heat or cold?*
Cold – you can catch cold easily.

646. *What do we always expect to find on at the cinema?*
The roof.

645. *Which animal is it best to be on a cold day?*
A little otter.

644. *Why is the apple tree crying?*
Because people are always picking on him.

643. *What has one horn and gives milk?*
A milk lorry.

642. *'Waiter, this egg is bad.'*
'Don't blame me, I only laid the table.'

641. Did you hear about the cannibal who came home to find his wife chopping up snakes and a very small man?
'Oh no,' he sighed. 'Not snake and pygmy pie again.'

640. PSYCHIATRIST TO HIS SECRETARY: Just say that we are very busy, *not*, 'It's like a madhouse here'.

639. The house we stayed in while we were on holiday last year was only a stone's throw from the beach. It was easy to find – all the windows were broken.

638. Did you hear about the little boy whose nose was eleven inches long? He was worried that if it grew any longer it would turn into a foot.

637. *What is a polygon?*
A dead parrot.

636. *What did the woodman's wife say to him one day?*
'There aren't many chopping days to go before Christmas.'

635. *What gets wetter the more it dries?*
A towel.

634. *Who gets the sack every time he goes to work?*
The postman.

633. *What is green, bent and indestructible?*
The Six Million Dollar Cucumber.

632. *What do you call the panic you feel when you are surrounded by sharks?*
Jawstrophobia.

631. FATHER: *I see from your school report that you are not doing so well in history.*
SON: It's not my fault. The teacher always asks me about things that happened before I was born.

630. NIT: *Haven't I seen your face somewhere else?*
WIT: I don't think so. It's always been between my ears.

629. *What's the difference between a dog and a flea?*
A dog can have fleas, but a flea can't have dogs!

628. *'How much after midnight is it?'*
'I don't know, my watch only goes as high as twelve.'

627. *What did the Russian Tarzan say when he met a crane?*
'Me Tarzan. Ukraine.'

626. *Why does a baker do his work?*
Just for the dough.

625. *Why did the show-off throw a bucket of water out of the window?*
He wanted to make a big splash.

624. *What goes 'da-dit-dit croak, da-dit-dit croak'?*
A Morse Toad.

623. *What goes round a yard but does not move?*
A fence.

622. *What's the difference between a biscuit and an elephant?*
You can't dip an elephant in your tea.

621. *Knock, knock.*
Who's there?
Howie.
Howie who?
I'm okay, how are you?

620. *If kings like to sit on gold, who likes to sit on Silver?*
      The Lone Ranger.

619. *How long were you in the Army?*
      About six feet, three and a half inches.

618. *When is an operation funny?*
      When it leaves the patient in stitches.

617. *What did the chimney sweep say when asked if he
          liked his work?*
      It soots me.

616. Bulldog for sale. Eats anything. Very fond of
      children.

615. *What's fast, bald and takes pictures?*
A Kojak Instamatic.

614. *What did the Eskimo say after he'd finished building his igloo?*
'Ours is an ice (a nice) house, ours is.'

613. *What is green, curly and religious?*
Lettuce pray.

612. *What do you give an elephant who is exhausted?*
Trunkquillisers.

611. *Why did the blind chicken cross the road?*
To get to the Birds Eye shop.

610. My Dad is so short-sighted he can't get to sleep unless he counts elephants.

609. *Which two letters of the alphabet are worn out?*
D. K. (decay)

608. *What is hairy and coughs?*
A coconut with a cold.

607. *What is the hardest thing about learning to ride a bike?*
The road.

606. *What do you call a motorcycle thief?*
A Honda-taker.

605. *Why are vampires unpopular?*
Because they are a pain in the neck.

604. *What animal talks a lot?*
A yak.

603. *What stays hot in a fridge?*
Mustard.

602. The home of a swallow is in the stomach.

601. *What fish sings songs?*
Tuna fish.

600. *What is sandpaper?*
An Irishman's map of the desert.

599. *Why did the chicken cross the road?*
Because he saw the zebra crossing.

598. *How do you know if an elephant has been in your fridge?*
You'll see footprints in the butter.

597. *What's green and prickly and goes up and down?*
A gooseberry in a lift.

596. *How would you know your dustbin was full of toadstools?*
Because there wouldn't be mushroom inside.

595. *Where does a sheep get his hair cut?*
At a baa-baa shop.

594. *What would you call a grandfather clock?*
An old timer.

593. Humpty Dumpty sat on a wall,
      Humpty Dumpty had a great fall,
      All the king's horses and all the king's men
      Had scrambled egg again.

592. *When do you swallow your words?*
      When you eat alphabet soup.

591. *Why are cabbages generous?*
      Because they have big hearts.

590. *What can you make that nobody else can see?*
      A noise.

589. *How does the fireplace feel when you fill it with coal?*
      Grate-ful, of course.

588. *If a boy ate his mother and father, what would that
          make him?*
      An orphan.

587. *I have a head and a tail but no body. What am I?*
      A penny.

586. *When is an apple not an apple?*
      When it's a crab.

585. *What grows in the jungle, makes great sandwiches
          and should always be avoided?*
      A hambush.

584. *How do you write a letter to a fish?*
      Just drop him a line.

583. *If a lion was following you what steps would you take?*
The longest steps possible.

582. *What is Chinese and deadly?*
Chop sueycide.

581. *Why are people who read on train journeys very clever?*
Because they can read between the lines.

580. *What starts with T, ends with T and is full of T?*
A teapot.

579. *Knock, knock.*
Who's there?
Boo.
Boo who?
I'll tell you when you stop crying.

578. *What fish is very musical?*
A piano-tuna.

577. *What did one clover say to the other clover?*
Take me to your weeder.

576. *If a butcher was 7 feet tall and wore size 16 shoes,
what would he weigh?*
Meat, of course.

575. *What happens when two French prams collide?*
You have a crêche.

574. *What did the dying pup say?*
Well, I'll be doggone.

573. *What do kangaroos have that no other animals have?*
Little kangaroos.

572. *Why do vampires go to Earls Court?*
For the Bat Show, of course.

571. *What lies at the bottom of the sea and shivers?*
A nervous wreck.

570. *What did Tennessee?*
He saw what Arkansas.

569. *Which trees do hands grow on?*
Palm trees.

568. 'I've borrowed my neighbour's bagpipes.'
'But you can't play them.'
'I know, but neither can he while I've got them.'

567. *What is a forum?*
Two-um plus two-um.

566. *How does a Hawaiian baritone laugh?*
A – lo – ha.

565. *Why do undertakers go to Wembley?*
For the Hearse of the Year Show.

564. LAZY LEN: *Go outside and see if it's raining.*
LITTLE JOHN: I've got a better idea. Call the dog in and
see if he's wet.

563. *If a buttercup is yellow, what colour is a hiccup?*
Burple.

562. *What is the definition of a robin?*
A bird that steals.

561. MOTHER TO LITTLE BOY: How many millions of times
have I told you *not* to exaggerate?

560. *What game do judges play?*
Tennis – because it's played on courts.

559. *Which town in Britain sells bad meat?*
Oldham (old ham).

558. *When is a shaggy dog most likely to enter a house?*
When the door is open.

557. *When is a sailor not a sailor?*
When he's aboard.

556. *What room has no floor, ceiling, windows or doors?*
A mushroom.

555. *How do you use an Egyptian doorbell?*
Toot-and-come-in.

554. *Knock, knock.*
Who's there?
Oswald.
Oswald who?
Oswald my bubble gum.

553. Did you hear about the girl who was so shy she went into a cupboard to change her mind.

552. *What did the baby porcupine say when it backed into a cactus?*
'Is that you, Mother?'

551. *What did the tablecloth say to the table?*
'Don't move, I've got you covered.'

550. *What's the difference between a hill and a pill?*
A hill is hard to get up and a pill is hard to get down.

549. *Where would two motorists have a swordfight?*
On a duel carriageway.

548. *What do you call Scottish shellfish?*
The Clam Mactavish.

547. *What did the stag say to his children?*
'Hurry up, deer.'

546. FIRST ANGEL: *You can tell that Smithy was a careful driver when he was on earth.*
SECOND ANGEL: How's that?
FIRST ANGEL: *Because now he's up here, he's asked to be fitted with wing mirrors.*

545. PATIENT: *Doctor, I'm having trouble with my breathing.*
DOCTOR: I'll see if I can give you something to stop that.

544. *If you want to be rich, why should you keep your mouth shut?*
Because silence is golden.

543. *Why do vampires sleep in coffins?*
Because of the low rent.

542. *'Call me a taxi, my good man.'*
'Certainly, Sir. You're a taxi.'

541. Psychiatrists tell us that one out of four people is mentally ill. So check your friends – if three of them seem okay, you're the one.

540. Sign in front of cemetery: DUE TO A STRIKE, GRAVEDIGGING WILL BE DONE BY A SKELETON CREW.

539. MOTHER: *Johnny, stop reaching across the table. Haven't you got a tongue?*
JOHNNY: Yes, but my arm is longer.

538. *Why did the little boy always stand on a ladder when he sang his song?*
So he could reach the high notes.

537. *What is the difference between a blueberry and an elephant?*
A blueberry is blue.

536. *I think Joan is an absolute angel.*
Yes, you can tell by the way she harps on things.

535. CUSTOMER: *Are these seeds quick-growing?*
SHOP ASSISTANT: I'll say, Sir. After planting them, jump well clear.

534. *Where do rabbits obtain planning permission for new homes?*
From the Burrow Surveyor.

533. *Why did the elephants quit the circus?*
They got tired of working for peanuts.

532. *Simple Simon decided to walk home.*
'Why don't you take the bus?' asked his friend.
'Because my mother will make me take it back.'
replied Simon.

531. *What did the five-hundred-pound mouse say when it walked into the alley?*
'Here, kitty, kitty, kitty.'

530. *How do people eat cheese in Wales?*
Caerphilly.

529. *Have you heard about Will Knot?*
He signs his name WON'T.

528. *What do you get if you cross an elephant with a goldfish?*
Swimming trunks.

527. *What is the difference between twice twenty-two and twice two and twenty?*
The first is 44, and the second is 24.

526. *When is a department store like a boat?*
When it has sales.

525. *When is a boat like a heap of snow?*
When it is adrift.

524. *In what ball can you carry your shopping?*
A basketball.

523. *What's grey and lights up?*
An electric elephant.

522. People who cough loudly never go to the doctor – they go to the cinema.

521. *What kind of clock is crazy?*
A cuckoo clock.

520. *What is the definition of guerilla warfare?*
Monkeys throwing coconuts at each other.

519. TEACHER: *What is an octopus?*
SILLY BILLY (after giving the question quite a bit of
thought): An eight-sided cat.

518. *What holds the moon up?*
Moon-beams, of course.

517. *What did the wolf-man eat after he had his teeth
taken out?*
The dentist.

516. *Do bright eyes indicate curiosity?*
No, but black ones do.

515. *Did Adam and Eve ever have a date?*
No, they had an apple.

514. *How can you tell the colour of plums?*
Use a green gauge.

513. Did you hear about the Irishman who drove his car
into a lake? He was trying to dip his headlights.

512. *'Doctor, I keep thinking there are two of me.'*
'Don't both speak at once.'

511. I wouldn't say that my wife was a bad cook, but
our dustbin has ulcers.

510. We were going to have some Morris Dancing, but
Morris couldn't come.

509. *What did one sole say to the other?*
'Watch out, there are two heels following us.'

508. *What is brown and sounds like a bell?*
Dung!

507. *Where does Tarzan get his clothes?*
From a jungle sale.

506. *What do you call the angry dolphins?*
Cross porpoises.

505. *What is a ringleader?*
The first one in the bathtub.

504. *What's red and goes putt, putt, putt?*
An outboard apple.

503. FIRST CANNIBAL: *How do you know our new missionary has been eaten?*
SECOND CANNIBAL: I've got inside information.

502. *Where are there no fat people?*
In Finland.

501. *When is the ocean like a piece of string?*
When a ship makes knots in it.

500. *'Doctor, I keep talking to myself.'*
'I wondered why you were looking so bored.'

499. *Why do white sheep eat more than black ones?*
Because there are more of them in the world.

498. SIMPLETON: *This match won't light.*
MAN: What's the matter with it?
SIMPLETON: *I don't know, it worked a minute ago.*

497. MOTHER: *Sally, don't you know you are not supposed to eat with your knife?*
SALLY: I know, but my fork leaks.

496. *Why was the skeleton a coward?*
Because he had no guts.

495. *How do elephants dive into swimming pools?*
Head first.

494. There is always a long queue of people at this theatre
– trying to get out.

493. *Which side of an apple pie is the left side?*
The part that isn't eaten.

492. MRS JONES: *Have you told your little boy not to go
around imitating me?*
MRS SMITH: Yes, I have. I told him not to act like an
idiot.

491. *What do you use to cut through giant waves?*
A sea-saw.

490. *What do you get if you cross a miserable man with a
space-ship?*
A moan-rocket.

489. *What is a cannibal's favourite kind of soup?*
One with plenty of body in it.

488. *What is rhubarb?*
Celery with high blood pressure.

487. The largest women in the USA are Mrs Sippy and
Miss Oury.

486. *Why don't you go into the jungle after seven o'clock?*
Because of elephants falling out of trees.

485. *What did the window say to the venetian blind?*
'If it weren't for you, it would be curtains for me.'

484. *'Today I saw a baby who had put on five kilos in
weight in two weeks by drinking elephant's milk.'*
'Whose baby was it?'
'The elephant's.'

483. *Why did the farmer call his rooster 'Robinson'?*
Because he crew so.

482. CUSTOMER: *Waiter, there's a fly in my soup.*
WAITER: No, Sir, that's the chef – the last customer was a witch doctor.

481. *Knock, knock.*
Who's there?
Doughnut.
Doughnut who?
Doughnut ask me silly questions.

480. *How do you spell mouse-trap in three letters?*
C – A – T.

479. *What swings about a sweet-shop, yodelling?*
Tarzipan.

478. *What happens if you fail to pay an exorcist?*
You get repossessed.

477. *Why do elephants have wrinkled knees?*
From playing marbles.

476. *What's big, black, and eats rocks?*
A big, black rock-eater.

475. *Why did the monster want to buy a sea-horse?*
So he could play water polo.

474. AUNTY: *What are you going to give your baby sister for Christmas, Tommy?*
TOMMY: I'm not sure yet. I gave her the measles last Christmas.

473. *What do you fire from underwater guns?*
Sea-shells.

472. *Where do cowboys keep their supply of water?*
In their ten-gallon hats.

471. *Why are painted portraits like a tin of sardines?*
Because they are usually done in oils.

470. *How do you stop a herd of elephants from charging?*
Take away their credit cards.

469. *What goes tick, tick, woof?*
A watch dog.

468. *What do you get if you cross an elephant with a bus driver?*
A trunk an' driver.

467. CUSTOMER: *There's a dead fly in my soup.*
WAITER: Not so loud, Sir, or they will all want one.

466. *What is the difference between a woman and an umbrella?*
You can shut up an umbrella.

465. CUSTOMER: *There is something wrong with these hot dogs.*
WAITER: What do you want me to do? I'm a waiter, not a vet.

464. *If you put three ducks into a wooden crate, what would you have?*
A box of quackers.

463. *On which side does a chicken have most feathers?*
On the outside.

462. Did you hear about the group of city boys who were out for a walk in the country? They came across a pile of empty milk bottles and thought they'd found a cow's nest.

461. *How do you make a cigarette lighter?*
Take out the tobacco.

460. *What fish makes a good pudding?*
A jellyfish.

459. TOM: *It's raining cats and dogs today.*
      DICK: I know. I just stepped into a poodle.

458. EDUCATED ARCHIE: *When did Caesar reign?*
      DIZZY DILYS: I didn't know he rained.
      EDUCATED ARCHIE: *Of course. Didn't they hail him?*

457. *What is a piece of pie called in Italian?*
      A pizza pie.

456. JACK: *What do you sell?*
      JILL: Salt.
      JACK: *I'm a salt-seller too.*
      JILL: Shake.

455. *What is everybody in the world doing at the same time?*
      Growing older.

454. *What is the weakest animal in the world?*
      A frog. He will croak if you touch him.

453. *What box can never keep a secret?*
      A chatterbox.

452. *Do you believe in striking children?*
      Only in self-defence.

451. *Which birds are religious?*
      Birds of prey.

450. My husband has got such a long face that his barber
      charges him double for shaving it.

449. *How can you tell when an elephant is under your bed?*
Your nose touches the ceiling.

448. *Why is a sleeping baby like a hijack?*
Because it's a kid-napping.

447. *What do they call private detectives in Fairyland?*
Sherlock Gnomes.

446. JOEY: *Where do all the bugs go in winter?*
ZOE: Search me.
JOEY: *No thanks. I just wanted to know.*

445. *What is the definition of mistletoe?*
It's what astronauts get instead of athlete's foot (missile toe).

444. *Knock, knock.*
Who's there?
Izzie.
Izzie who?
Izzie at the door? You'd better answer it.

443. *Why did the boy ask his father to sit in the refrigerator?*
Because he wanted ice-cold pop!

442. *What's a quick snack for a cannibal?*
A sandwich-man.

441. BOATING LAKE ATTENDANT: Come in, Number 9. Come in, Number 9. Oh, are you in trouble, Number 6?

440. If you want to save money on pet food, get a polar bear; he lives on ice.

439. *Why is a heart like a policeman?*
Because it has a regular beat.

438. *What do you call Batman and Robin when they have been run over by a steam-roller?*
Flatman and Ribbon.

437. ANGRY MUM: *Why did you put this frog in your sister's bed?*
NAUGHTY CHILD: Because I couldn't find a mouse.

436. MUM: *Dad, aren't you supposed to take Jimmy to the zoo today?*
DAD: Not me! If the zoo wants him they can come and get him.

435. *If your nose runs and your feet smell, what's wrong with you?*
You're built upside-down.

434. *Is it true that carrots are good for the eyesight?*
Well, you never see rabbits wearing glasses.

432. My husband is such a hypochondriac that he refused to kiss me until I bought a lipstick with penicillin in it.

431. *What happens before a bird grows up?*
It grows down.

430. *What do you call a Scotsman who delivers school
meals?*
Dinner Ken.

429. ANDREW: *Did the music teacher really say your voice
was out of this world?*
PETER: Not exactly. She said it was unearthly.

428. *What is a prickly pear?*
Two porcupines.

427. *Why did the moron take a bicycle to bed?*
Because he didn't want to walk in his sleep.

426. *What is the definition of seasickness?*
It's what a doctor does all day.

425. *What animal drives an automobile?*
A road hog.

424. *What did Noah say to his sons as they were fishing
from the side of the ark?*
'Go easy with the bait, boys. I only have *two* worms.'

423. MOTHER: *Johnny's teacher says he ought to have an
encyclopaedia.*
FATHER: Let him walk to school the same as I did.

422. I used to be a taxi driver, but I drove all my
customers away.

421. *Knock, knock.*
Who's there?
Lee.
Lee who?
Lee me alone, I have a headache.

420. *What sign does an Irish window cleaner put at the top
of his ladder?*
STOP.

419. *How do you top a car?*
Tep on the brake, tupid.

418. LITTLE GIRL: *Mummy, Mummy, that boy next door
broke my dolly.*
MUMMY: How did he do that, dear?
LITTLE GIRL: *I hit him over the head with it.*

417. Two frogs sat in a restaurant. One gave the waiter his order but the other frog just sat there saying nothing. Finally his friend asked him why he didn't order. 'I can't,' whispered the frog. 'I have a man in my throat.'

416. *What man shaves more than ten times daily?*
A barber.

415. *Who always goes to sleep with his shoes on?*
A horse.

414. FIRST UNDERTAKER: *How's business?*
SECOND UNDERTAKER: Same as usual – dead.

413. *Where do frogs leave their hats and coats?*
In the croakroom.

412. *Why did you give up tap dancing?*
I kept falling in the sink.

411. TIM: *How do you know your mum wants to get rid of you?*
KIM: Why else would she pack a road map with my lunch every day?

410. *What part of a fish weighs the most?*
The scales.

409. *What is a bird after he is four days old?*
Five days old.

408. *Why do elephants chew camphor balls?*
To keep the moths away from their trunks.

407. *What has four legs and a back but no body?*
A chair.

406. *What is the correct thing to do before the King of Trees?*
Bough (bow).

405. *If you crossed King Kong with a bell, what would you have?*
A ding-dong King Kong.

404. *What kind of bird would you find down a coal-pit?*
A mynah bird.

403. BARBER: *Your hair is getting grey, Sir.*
CUSTOMER: No wonder – hurry up.

402. *What did Cinderella say when her pictures didn't arrive?*
'Someday my prints will come.'

401. *Why were the elephants the last to leave the Ark?*
Because they had to pack their trunks.

400. PATIENT: *Doctor, I keep thinking I'm a dog.*
DOCTOR: How long has this been going on?
PATIENT: *Oh, ever since I was a puppy.*

399. *Where can everyone find money if they look for it?*
In the dictionary.

398. *Why are plants like very naughty boys?*
Because they need a stick to grow up straight.

397. *What can you use to stop a parrot from falling from his perch?*
Polly-Grip.

396. *Why did the little old man have a hundred clocks around the house?*
Because he heard that time was valuable.

395. *What does a winner lose in a race?*
His breath.

394. *Do mountains have ears?*
Of course, they have mountaineers.

393. *Why do birds fly south in the winter?*
Because it's too far to walk.

392. *What do you get when you cross a tin of cocoa with an elk?*
A chocolate mousse.

391. Three boys were sharing the same bed, but it was so crowded that one of them decided to sleep on the floor. After a while, one of his friends told him he might as well get back into bed. 'There's lots more room now,' he said.

390. *How does the letter A help a deaf woman?*
Because it makes her hear.

389. BOASTFUL MAN (telling a story): *On my right hand was a lion, on my left was a tiger, and in front and at the back of me were wild elephants . . .*
GULLIBLE GIRL: What happened next?
BOASTFUL MAN: *The merry-go-round stopped and I had to get off.*

388. FIRST WOODWORM: *How's life with you these days?*
SECOND WOODWORM: Oh, very boring.

387. Did you hear about the clergyman who had a flashing orange nose and was known as a Belisha Deacon?

386. HUSBAND: *The coffee tastes terrible.*
WIFE: I can't understand why. It's fresh. I made it in my pyjamas.
HUSBAND: *No wonder it tastes funny.*

385. TIM: *What's the best thing to put into a pie?*
TOM: Your teeth.

384. **MAN IN PET SHOP:** *I do like this dog but his legs are too short.*
SALESMAN: Short, Sir? All four reach the floor.

383. *What is the definition of an actor?*
Someone who tries to be everyone but himself.

382. *What has fifty heads and fifty tails?*
Fifty pennies.

381. *What person has the loudest voice?*
The ice-cream (I scream) man.

380. *Why did the old man lose his hair?*
Through worrying about losing his hair.

379. *Where do they collect recordings of English cows?*
In the British Mooseum, of course.

378. *Why do vampires brush their teeth?*
To stop bat breath.

377. *What is the definition of sideburns?*
What you get when your electric blanket is too hot.

376. **FARMER:** *Why are you running a steamroller over the potato patch?*
YOKEL: Because I want mashed poatoes.

375. *Knock, knock.*
Who's there?
Snow.
Snow who?
Snow use, I've forgotten my name again.

374. *What is the best way to talk to a monster?*
Long distance.

373. *What makes the letter T so important to a stick insect?*
Because without it, it would be a sick insect.

372. *What goes from branch to branch and wears a bowler hat?*
A bank manager.

371. *Where do spirits stay when they go on holiday?*
At ghost houses.

370. SIMPLE SARAH: Mum, there's a man at the door collecting for the old folk's home. Shall I give him Grandad?

369. *What kind of cat do you always find in a library?*
A cat-alogue.

368. *What is Count Dracula's favourite snack?*
A fangfurter.

367. *What is the best way to get out from under an elephant?*
Wait until he goes away.

366. *When things go wrong, what can you always count on?*
Your fingers.

365. *What is the definition of intense?*
A place where Boy Scouts sleep.

364. 'Waiter, there's a fly in my soup.'
'Oh dear, it must have committed insecticide!'

363. JUNIOR: *Dad, can I have another glass of water before I go to sleep?*
DAD: But this is your tenth.
JUNIOR: *I know, but my room is on fire.*

362. *What do spies do after they've eaten some microfilm?*
Wait and see what develops.

361. *What goes up in the air white and comes down yellow and white?*
An egg.

360. *Why is a rabbit's nose always shiny?*
Because its powder puff is on the wrong end.

359. *'There's a man outside to see you with a funny face.'*
'Well, tell him I've already got one.'

358. *What goes up when the rain comes down?*
An umbrella.

357. *What's yellow and always points north?*
A magnetic banana.

356. *What is the difference between a postage stamp and a girl?*
One is a mail fee and the other a female.

355. POLICEMAN: *Why are you driving your car in reverse?*
DAFT MOTORIST: Because I know my Highway Code backwards.

354. **TEACHER** (to Little Billy): *When the barometer falls, what does that mean?*
   LITTLE BILLY: That the nail's come out of the wall, Miss.

353. If you went to a skeleton's ball, would you have a rattling good time?

352. *Who tracks down lost vicars?*
   The Bureau of Missing Parsons.

351. *Where do the Chinese make motor-car horns?*
   Hong King.

350. *How do rabbits keep their fur neat and tidy?*
They use a harebrush.

349. *What is worse than a giraffe with a sore throat?*
A centipede with sore feet.

348. *Why are children like a flannel?*
Because they shrink from washing.

347. *If two's company and three's a crowd, what is four and five?*
Nine.

346. *Did you hear about the fight on the train?*
Yes. The inspector punched a ticket.

345. *Did you hear about the blind man who picked up a hammer and saw?*
No, but I know about the dumb man who picked up a wheel and spoke.

344. *What gadget do we use to see through a wall?*
A window.

343. My wife treats me like an idol. She feeds me with burnt offerings three times a day.

342. *What is the correct name for a shish kabob?*
A shish ka-Robert.

341. Is a drunken ghost a methylated spirit?

340. *What does a monster do when he loses a hand?*
Goes to a second-hand store.

339. Two little girls were paddling in the sea at Brighton when one sad to the other: 'Ooh, ain't your feet dirty!'
'Yes,' said the other, 'we didn't come last year.'

338. *Knock, knock.*
Who's there?
Dishes.
Dishes who?
Dishes the FBI. Open up.

337. *Why are dentists artistic?*
Because they are good at drawing teeth.

336. *What did Lot do when his wife got turned into a block of salt?*
He put her in the cellar.

335. *What's the last thing you take off before you go to bed?*
Your feet off the floor.

334. *'Doctor, I have this terrible problem. I keep stealing things.'*
'Have you taken anything for it?'

333. Did you hear the one about the young ghost who got very scared whenever he listened to human stories?

332. JACK: *I've got a parrot that can really count.*
JILL: Is that so?
JACK: *Yes, I asked him what two take away two was and he said nothing.*

331. *What sort of fur would you get from a grizzly bear?*
As fur away as possible.

330. *What did one ear say to the other?*
Between you and me we need a haircut.

329. CUSTOMER: *Waiter, there's a dead fly in my soup.*
WAITER: What do you want me to do – give it the kiss
of life?

328. *What's the best thing for water on the knee?*
Drainpipe trousers.

327. WOMAN TO STOREKEEPER: If my husband doesn't
like this mink coat will you refuse to take it back?

326. *What kind of bow can't be tied?*
A rainbow.

325. *'I'm very sorry, but I have just run over your cat and I
would like to replace it.'*
'How are you at catching mice?'

324. My scarecrow is so good at scaring the birds away that
they've brought back all the seed they stole last
week.

323. *What do you get if a cat swallows a ball of wool?*
Mittens.

322. PATIENT: *Doctor, have you got something for my
liver?*
DOCTOR: How about some onions?

321. *What is worse than finding a maggot in the apple you're eating?*
Finding half a maggot.

320. TEACHER: *What can you tell me about the Dead Sea?*
JOHNNY: I didn't even know it was ill.

319. *When is a window like a star?*
When it's a skylight.

318. *Who brings the Christmas presents to the police stations?*
Santa Clues.

317. *What goes dit-da-dit-dit-da-dit-bzzzzz and then bites you?*
A morsequito.

316. *What do you call a mischievous egg?*
A practical yolker.

315. *What disease do most nudists suffer from?*
Clothestrophobia.

314. *What happens when a flea gets really angry?*
He gets hopping mad.

313. *What did the man say when he heard that the price of candles had doubled?*
That's candalous (scandalous).

312. *Knock, knock.*
Who's there?
Dismay.
Dismay who?
Dismay be a joke, but it doesn't make me laugh.

311. *How do you know peanuts are fattening?*
Have you ever seen a skinny elephant?

310. *What kind of coat can you put on wet?*
A coat of paint.

309. FIRST POLICEMAN: *The thief got away then? Did you put guards on all the exits?*
SECOND POLICEMAN: Of course we did. But he tricked us and went out through an entrance.

308. TEACHER: *What kind of leather makes the best shoes?*
TINA: I don't know, but banana peels make the best slippers.

307. Did you hear about the cannibal who kept getting chronic indigestion? He ate people who disagreed with him.

306. *How did Little Bo-Peep lose her sheep?*
She had a crook with her.

305. *Why is your nose in the middle of your face?*
Because it is the scenter (centre).

304. Did you hear about the slow swimmer who could only crawl?

303. *What perks do policemen get?*
Truncheon vouchers.

302. *How often do aircraft of this type crash, Pilot?*
Only once, Madam.

301. *What makes the Tower of Pisa lean?*
It never eats.

300. 'This is r-r-rough!' said the dog as he slid on the grit.

299. *What is the best way to stop fish smelling?*
Cut off their noses.

298. *What is purple and crazy?*
A grape nut.

297. *What has eight feet and can sing?*
A quartet.

296. *Knock, knock.*
Who's there?
Minnie.
Minnie who?
No, not Minnie who – Minnehaha.

295. ELSIE: *I'm homesick.*
JOAN: But this is your home.
ELSIE: *I know and I'm sick of it.*

294. CUSTOMER: *How much for a haircut?*
BARBER: Seventy-five pence.
CUSTOMER: *How much for a shave?*
BARBER: Fifty pence.
CUSTOMER: *Okay, shave my head.*

293. *Which floats the best, tin or stainless steel?*
Tin. Stainless steel sinks.

292. Hear about the fight in the fish and chip shop?
A lot of fish got battered.

291. *What's white outside, green inside and hops?*
A frog sandwich.

290. *What kind of bow can't be tied?*
A rainbow.

289. *Who is it that everyone listens to but nobody
    believes?*
The weather man.

288. *Who designed the first raincoat?*
Anna Rack.

287. There is now a new deodorant on the market called 'Vanish'. You spray it on and disappear. That way no one knows where the smell is coming from.

286. *Why is this station called Fish Hook?*
Because it's the end of the line.

285. *What is a mosquito with the itch?*
A jitterbug.

284. *Why was the farmer cross?*
Because someone trod on his corn.

283. Did you hear about the two blood cells?
They loved in vein.

282. *What's green and holds up stage-coaches?*
Dick Gherkin.

281. *What kind of pen does Kojak use?*
A bald-point pen.

280. *Why are elephants so wrinkled?*
Have you ever tried ironing one?

279. *How many feet are there in a yard?*
That depends on how many people there are in the yard.

278. *When does a chair dislike you most?*
When it cannot bear you.

277. *What's white, furry, and smells of peppermint?*
A polo bear.

276. A flea and a fly in a flue
Were imprisoned, so what could they do?
Said the fly, 'Let us flee!'
Said the flea, 'Let us fly!'
So they flew through a flaw in the flue.

275. *Why do elephants paint the soles of their feet yellow?*
So they can float upside down in custard, without
being seen.

274. NIT WIT: *I call my dog Isaiah.*
WIT NIT: Why do you call your dog Isaiah?
NIT WIT: *Because one eye's 'igher than the other.*

273. *Why did the wagon train stop in the middle of the prairie?*
Because it had Injun trouble.

272. *Knock, knock.*
Who's there?
Cows.
Cows who?
Cows go 'moo', not 'who'.

271. *What girl's name is like a letter?*
Kay.

270. A pedestrian is someone who can be reached easily by car.

269. *Which two types of fish do you need to make a shoe?*
Sole and 'eel.

268. MAN: *How does it feel to hurtle through space?*
ASTRONAUT: It hurtles!

267. *What is it that you can't see but is always before you?*
The future.

266. FARMER: *Where's that donkey I told you to take out and have shod?*
YOKEL: Oh, did you say shod? I thought you said shot!

265. Did you hear about the cat who won a milk-drinking contest? It lapped the field.

264. *What do ghosts take for a bad cold?*
Coffin drops.

263. MOLLY: *Do you like the new doctor?*
POLLY: Oh yes. He's so sympathetic that he makes
you feel really ill.

262. *When you look around on a cold winter's day, what
do you see on every hand?*
A glove.

261. Did you hear about the man who got so fed up
reading that smoking was bad for the health that he
immediately gave up reading?

260. And did you also hear about the man who was sent to
prison for something he didn't do – he didn't jump
into the get-away car fast enough?

259. *What does a queen do when she burps?*
She issues a royal pardon.

258. JUDGE TO CRIMINAL: *How plead you, guilty or not
guilty?*
CRIMINAL: I won't know till I've heard the evidence.

257. *What is insurance?*
What you pay for now so that you'll have nothing to
worry about when you are dead.

256. *When do you go as fast as Concorde?*
When you are in it.

255. *What food does a vampire dislike most?*
Steak (stake).

254. *What lurks at the bottom of the sea and makes you an offer you can't refuse?*
The Codfather.

253. *What occurs in every minute, twice in a moment, and yet never in a thousand years?*
The letter M.

252. PASSENGER: *How can I make sure that the trains are running on time?*
PORTER: Just before a train is due, put your watch on the railway line.

251. *Why did Jane divorce Tarzan?*
He became too big a swinger.

250. *Knock, knock.*
Who's there?
Arthur.
Arthur who?
Arthur any more biscuits in the tin?

249. CUSTOMER: *Waiter, I'd like an elephant sandwich.*
WAITER: I'm very sorry, Sir, but we don't do elephant sandwiches.
CUSTOMER: *Why not?*
WAITER: Because we haven't any bread.

248. Two astronauts went into a pub on the moon, but they didn't stay long. They said it had no atmosphere.

247. TEACHER: *If there were a dozen flies on my desk and I swatted one, how many would be left?*
BRIGHT PUPIL: The dead one.

246. *How do you save a drowning mouse?*
Give it mouse to mouse resuscitation.

245. *Why don't elephants ride bicycles?*
Because their thumbs are too big to work the bell.

244. *How do you get four giraffes in a Mini?*
You can't. It's full up with elephants.

243. DOCTOR'S RECEPTIONIST: *You'll find the new doctor very funny – he'll have you in stitches.*
PATIENT: I hope not. I only came for a check-up.

242. *When do most highway robberies happen?*
At Turpin time.

241. Did you know about the dancer who became a spy?
His phone was tapped.

240. *When is an artist unhappy?*
When he draws a long face.

239. *Why are fish well educated?*
Because they travel in schools.

238. *How do you start a bear race?*
Ready, teddy, go!

237. *Why did Johnny give one of the new boys next door a black eye?*
Because they were identical twins and he wanted to be able to tell them apart.

236. *Which is heavier, a half or a full moon?*
A half moon, because the full moon is lighter.

235. *What is the definition of 'paralyse'?*
Two fibs.

234. *What happened when the boy monster met the girl monster?*
They fell in love at first fright.

233. A team of doctors has just discovered a cure for which there is no disease.

232. *'Now you see me, now you don't. What am I?'*
'A black cat on a zebra crossing.'

231. *Why did the Irishman sew labels saying 'wool' in all his cotton clothing?*
He wanted to fool the moths.

230. *What do you give a seasick elephant?*
Lots of room.

229. FATHER: *How did that window get broken?*
SON: I was cleaning my catapult and it went off by accident.

228. TOM: *I've been hunting with my dad. We brought back four rabbits and a potfor.*
TIM: What's a potfor?
TOM: *To cook the rabbits in.*

227. 'These mothballs you sold me are no good.'
'Why not?'
'I haven't hit a single moth yet.'

226. What's pink, old, and belongs to Grandad?
Grandma.

225. MUSIC TEACHER: Is there anything special you'd like
to be able to play?
PUPIL: Yes, Miss. Truant.

224. Why do artists never need to be short of money?
Because they can always draw a cheque.

223. Two creatures from Outer Space landed by a traffic
light.
'I saw her first,' said one.
'So what?' said the other. 'I'm the one she winked at.'

222. Which fish wears spurs and a cowboy hat?
Billy the Cod.

221. DUFFY: What's that book the orchestra keeps looking
at?
MUFFY: That's the score.
DUFFY: Really? Who's winning?

220. Why is an empty room like a room full of married
people?
Because there isn't a single person in it.

219. What wears shoes but has no feet?
The pavement.

218. FIRST NEIGHBOUR: *Do you believe in free speech?*
SECOND NEIGHBOUR: Of course I do.
FIRST NEIGHBOUR: *Good. Can I use your telephone?*

217. *What time is it when it's halfway between the 'tick' and the 'tock'?*
Half past tick o'tock.

216. *How does an octopus go to war?*
Armed.

215. *Why did Batman go to the pet shop?*
To buy a robin.

214. *Where does a ghost train stop?*
At a manifestation.

213. *How can you tell if a train has gone past?*
By the tracks it leaves.

212. My brother is famous for his bird impressions!
He eats worms.

211. ENGLISHMAN: *And is this your most charming wife?*
IRISHMAN: No, it's the only one I've got.

210. *What's a brass band?*
A ring that turns your finger green.

209. *Which Red Indian tribe had the most lawyers?*
The Sioux.

208. The thunder god went for a ride on his favourite
     horse.
     'I'm Thor!' he cried.
     The horse replied: 'Don't be thilly, you forgot your
     thaddle.'

207. *A dollar and a cent fell out of a pocket. The cent
     rolled along the gutter and fell down the drain.
     Why did't the dollar follow?*
     Because it had more cents (sense).

206. PATIENT: *Doctor, how can I stop myself sleep-
     walking?*
     DOCTOR: Sprinkle drawing pins on your bedroom
     floor.

205. *What is a very hard subject?*
     The study of rocks.

204. *What comes down but can never go up?*
     The rain.

203. *Why does the Indian wear feathers in his hair?*
     To keep his wigwam.

202. *Why is a horse like a cricket match?*
     Because it gets stopped by the rein (rain).

201. *Knock, knock.*
     Who's there?
     Acid.
     Acid who?
     Acid down and be quiet.

200. TOM: *Did you ever see the Catskill Mountains?*
JERRY: No, but I've seen them kill mice.

199. CUSTOMER: *I'll have a hamburger, please.*
WAITER: With pleasure.
CUSTOMER: *No, with pickles and onions.*

198. *Why do little birds in the nest always agree?*
Because they don't want to fall out.

197. *What is ignorance?*
When you don't know something and somebody finds
out.

196. A little girl said there was a new baby at her house.
'Has the baby come to stay?' she was asked.
'I think so,' she replied. 'He's taken all his things off!'

195. *What is an acquaintance?*
Someone you know well enough to borrow from, but
not well enough to lend to.

194. *What did Adam promise Eve after they were thrown
out of the Garden of Eden?*
They'd turn over a new leaf.

193. Simple Sam went into a shop to buy a pillow slip.
SALESWOMAN: *What size do you want?*
SIMPLE SAM: I don't know, but I wear a size 6 hat.

192. *How is a nursery like a dance hall?*
Because it's a bawlroom (ballroom).

191. *What did the big chimney say to the little chimney?*
'You're too young to smoke.'

190. *What do you get if you cross a yak with a parrot?*
A yakkety-yak.

189. *What do they call an extra-long hot dog?*
A frankfurther.

188. *Why can't the little boy play the piano?*
Because he can't reach that high.

187. *What do you call a man who's always wiring for money?*
An electrician.

186. *What has two heads, six feet, one tail and four ears?*
A man on horseback.

185. *What do you get if you cross a cat with a laughing hyena?*
A giggle puss.

184. *What is the definition of an ant?*
An insect that works hard but still finds time to go to all the picnics.

183. NEWS FLASH: Local man takes first prize in dog show.

182. LENNIE: *Why don't you buy Christmas seals?*
BENNIE: I don't know how to feed them.

181. 'I only weighed two kilograms when I was born,' said the man.
'Did you live?' asked his friend.
'Did I live? You should see me now!'

180. *Why can the world never come to an end?*
Because it's round.

179. *Why did the pig swill?*
Because he saw the barn dance.

178. Did you hear about the two potatoes who didn't see eye to eye? When one took his jacket off, the other thought he'd had his chips.

177. *Who wrote* Great Eggspectations?
Charles Chickens.

176.   FIRST CANNIBAL: *I don't like my mother-in-law.*
       SECOND CANNIBAL: Well, just eat the chips.

175.   *What should you take when you're run down?*
       The licence number of the elephant.

174.   *How do you know when you are getting old?*
       When the candles cost more than the cake.

173.   *What did one lift say to the other?*
       I think I'm coming down with something.

172.   GYPSY: Buy a lucky charm, Lady. Take away the
              curse I've just put on your house.

171.   *How would you get rid of a white elephant?*
       Put it in a jumble sale.

170.   A man watched his neighbour planting razor blades
       in his potato patch.
       'What are you hoping to grow?' he asked.
       'Chips,' came the reply.

169.   It was so hot where we spent our holiday last summer
       that we took turns sitting in each other's shadow.

168.   Did you hear about the man who threw away his
       shoes because he thought they were sticking their
       tongues out at him?

167.   *How does Jack Frost get to work?*
       By icicle, I guess.

166.   *What did the finger say to the thumb?*
       'People will say we're in glove.'

165. *What is long, red, and shoots rabbits?*
A double-barrelled carrot.

164. *What is curvy, yellow, and hangs about?*
A drip-dry banana.

163. NIGHT GUARD: *Halt, who goes there?*
VOICE: Well I never! How did you know my name?

162. *What do cats strive for?*
Purrfection.

161. *When is a chair like a fabric?*
When it is sat in (satin).

160. BOY: *My teacher shouted at me because I didn't know where the Pyramids were.*
FATHER: You remember where you put things next time.

159. MOTHER: *Why are you spanking Johnny, dear?*
FATHER: Because he's getting his school report tomorrow and I won't be here.

158. FIRST MAN: *What made you decide to become a parachute jumper?*
SECOND MAN: A plane with three dead engines.

157. *What squeals more loudly than a pig caught under a fence?*
Two pigs caught under a fence.

156. *What has tiny wings and is related to the camel?*
A hump-backed midge.

155. Did you hear about the absent-minded old man who put salt on the dog and patted the roast beef?

154. *Why is history the sweetest lesson?*
Because it's full of dates.

153. *Why is it dangerous to tell secrets in a field of wheat?*
Because corn has ears.

152. BIG GIRL: *Have you lived here all your life?*
LITTLE GIRL: No, not yet.

151. Did you hear about the girl who went to the corner to see the traffic jam? A truck came along and gave her a jar.

150. *Why are feet like ancient tales?*
Because they are leg-ends.

149. POSH LADY: *What can I do for you, my man?*
TRAMP: If you don't mind, Ma'am, I'd like a coat sewn on my button.

148. *What is the definition of glass work?*
What a window does for a living.

147. *What sea creature can add up?*
An octoplus.

146. *Why was the crab arrested?*
Because he was always pinching things.

145. *Why are army sergeants like dentists?*
Because they are both good at drilling.

144. *What is it that you need most in the long run?*
Your breath.

143. *'Waiter, there's a dead fly in my soup.'*
'Yes, it's the hot water that kills them.'

142. *When they take out your appendix it is called an appendectomy; when they take out your tonsils it is called a tonsillectomy; what is it called when they remove a growth from your head?*
A haircut.

141. ONE FORTUNE-TELLER TO THE OTHER: Grand weather we're having. It reminds me of the summer of 1996.

140. *Why did the zookeeper separate the gnus?*
He had good gnus and bad gnus.

139. *What is the most striking thing in the way of a mantle ornament?*
A clock.

138. *What part of a river can be eaten?*
The source and the current.

137. WIFE (at bedside of her sick husband): *Is there no hope, Doctor?*
DOCTOR: What are you hoping for?

136. I don't care who you are; get your reindeer off my roof!

135. *What weighs two tonnes and leaps around like a frog?*
A hoppy potamous.

134. *What is very tall, and goes 'Eef if of muf'?*
A backward giant.

133. CUSTOMER: *I'm looking for something cheap and nasty to give my mother-in-law as a present.*
SHOPKEEPER: I've got just the thing, Sir. My father-in-law.

132. *Have you read the Bible?*
No. I'm waiting for the film.

131. *What do you get when you cross a wild bird with a hiccup?*
Wild Bill Hiccup.

130. *What is a vampire's favourite soup?*
Alpha-bat (alphabet) soup.

129. *What is the proper way to address the King of Ghosts?*
Your Ghostliness.

128. *When is a piece of wood like a queen?*
When it's made into a ruler.

127. *What happens when the spare parts for Japanese cars fall out of an aeroplane?*
You could say it's raining Datsun cogs.

126. *'My Dad bought Mum a bone china teaset for her birthday.'*
'That was nice of him.'
'Yeah, but he only did it because he knew she wouldn't trust him to do the washing-up in case he broke it.'

125. MAN: *When you sold me this cat you told me it would be good for mice. It hasn't gone near them.*
PET-SHOP OWNER: Well, that's good for the mice, isn't it?

124. MOTHER (to her little boy): *I can't hear you saying your prayers.*
LITTLE BOY: Well, I'm not talking to you.

123. *How is cat food sold?*
So much purr can.

122. *Did all the animals on the ark come in pairs?*
No, the worms came in apples.

121. *Knock, knock.*
Who's there?
Cook.
Cook who?
Oh, that's the first one I've heard this year.

120. *What are the three best ways of spreading gossip?*
Telegraph, telephone – and tell a girl.

119. *What animal would you put in your washing machine?*
A wash and were-wolf.

118. MAN AT CONTROL TOWER: *Please tell me your height and position.*
POTTY PILOT: Oh, about 1.8 metres tall, and I'm sitting in the cockpit.

117. *Do you like your dentist?*
No, he bores me to tears.

116. *Why did the lawyer carry a ladder to work?*
     So he could take his case to a higher court.

115. *Who was Ivanhoe?*
     A Russian gardener.

114. *When can your coat pocket be empty, yet still have
     something in it?*
     When it has a hole.

113. *What would happen if everyone in the country had a
     pink car?*
     We'd be a pink carnation (car nation).

112. *What happened to the boy who ran away with the
     circus?*
     The police made him bring it back.

111. *'Once a week I take a milk bath.'*
     'Pasteurized?'
     'No, just up to my neck.'

110. TEACHER: *Your essay on* My Rabbit *is word for word
     the same as your sister's.*
     PUPIL: Well, it's the same rabbit, Sir.

109. *What animal can you never trust?*
     A cheetah.

108. *What did the pencil say to the rubber?*
     Take me to your ruler.

107. OPTICIAN: *What can you see out of that window?*
     MAN: I can only see the sun.
     OPTICIAN: *How far do you want to see, then?*

110

106. *What word is always pronounced wrong?*
Wrong.

105. *Did you hear about the Irish shoplifter?*
No.
He stole a free sample.

104. *And the one about the loaf of bread?*
Oh, crumbs.

103. *What do you get if you cross a cowboy with a popular meal?*
Hopalong Casserole.

102. *What game do elephants play in a Mini?*
Squash.

101. *What house weighs the least?*
A lighthouse.

100. TOPSY: *What's the difference between a lemon, a rhino, and a tube of glue?*
TURVEY: You can squeeze a lemon, but you can't squeeze a rhino. But what about the glue?
TOPSY: *I thought that's where you'd get stuck.*

99. *What is junk?*
Something you keep for years and then throw away just before you need it.

98. *If you cross a dog and cat, what would you get?*
An animal that chases itself.

97. *What is the strongest animal?*
A snail, because it carries its house on its back.

111

96. *Who are the best book-keepers?*
The people who never return the books you lend
them.

95. *What did the toothpaste say to the brush?*
'Give us a squeeze and I'll meet you outside the
Tube.'

94. *What's yellow, soft, and goes round and round?*
A long-playing omelette.

93. *What language does Jacques Cousteau speak?*
Fluid French.

92. *Did the rooster really fall in love with the hen at first
sight?*
Not really – she egged him on a bit.

91. *Why did the writer put his finger in the alphabet soup?*
He was trying to find the right words.

90. *Knock, knock.*
Who's there?
Datsun.
Datsun who?
Datsun old joke.

89. *What has fifty legs but can't walk?*
Twenty-five pairs of trousers.

88. *What is bought by the yard and worn by the foot?*
A carpet.

87. *What is the most expensive city in the world?*
Electricity.

86. Did you hear about the man who swallowed some
uranium by accident? He got atomic ache.

85. *Why is the Dracula family so close?*
Because blood is thicker than water.

84. *What cannot be seen but heard, and will only speak
when spoken to?*
An echo.

83. An adult is somebody who has stopped growing
except round the waist.

82. *'Waiter, is this tea or coffee? It tastes like petrol.'*
'Tea, Sir. The coffee tastes like paraffin.'

81. Did you hear about the human cannonball at the
circus? He got fired.

80. *Why did Princess's suitor not win her hand?*
Because he didn't suit her.

79. CUSTOMER (in shoe-shop): *I would like some
crocodile shoes, please.*
SALESMAN: Certainly, madam. What size shoe does
your crocodile take?

78. *If you broke your leg in two places, what would you
do?*
Stay out of those two places in future.

77. *Who rings the bell twice and then knocks down the door?*
The Avon gorilla.

76. *Why did the mother take the ink away from the baby?*
She knew he was too young to write a book.

75. *Where would you get a job playing a rubber trumpet?*
In an elastic band.

74. *What is black, out of its mind and sits in trees?*
A raven lunatic.

73. *What did one rock pool say to the other rock pool?*
Show us your mussels.

72. *Why did the baker stop making doughnuts?*
He got tired of the hole business.

71. *What has four legs and flies?*
A dead horse.

70. *What's the difference between a cat and a comma?*
A cat has claws at the end of his paws . . . and a
comma is a pause at the end of a clause.

69. *When should you put corn in your shoes?*
When you have pigeon toes.

68. *Why did the cow jump over the moon?*
Because there was no other way round to the other
side.

67. *What do you do with a green banana?*
Teach it something.

66. *What did Britain have before a blood bank?*
A Liverpool.

65. *What is the definition of defeat?*
What you walk on.

64. *When was beef the highest price it has ever been?*
When the cow jumped over the moon.

63. Two flies were playing football in a saucer. One said
to the other: 'We'll have to do better than this.
We're playing in the cup next week.'

62.   CUSTOMER: *Why are you giving me a lobster with only one claw?*
     WAITER: I'm sorry, Sir, but it was in a fight.
     CUSTOMER: *Well, take it away and give me the winner.*

61. *What happened to the man who discovered electricity?*
    He got a nasty shock.

60. *What's another name for a coffin?*
    A snuff box.

59. *What did the zoo-keeper see when the elephant squirted water from his trunk?*
    A jumbo jet.

58. Are you a man or a mouse? Squeak up.

57. Due to a strike at the meteorological office, there will be no weather in Britain tomorrow.

56. *When is an opera singer not an opera singer?*
    When she is a little hoarse.

55. *How many miles can a pirate ship travel?*
    Ten miles to the galleon.

54. *What is the definition of propaganda?*
    A real goose.

53. *Why did the Romans build straight roads?*
    Because they didn't want to drive their soldiers round the bend.

52. WITCH IN HOSPITAL: *Doctor, I feel so much better now.*

DOCTOR: That's good. You can get up for a spell this afternoon.

51. Did you hear about the man who lost his health because he was always drinking the health of others?

50. 'Are you any good at figures?' the butcher asked the boy who had applied for a job.

'Yes, Sir.'

'Right. What would two kilos of beef be at six pence a kilo?'

'Bad.'

'The job's yours.'

49. **MOTHER:** *How did you get Johnny to take his medicine without making a fuss?*
FATHER: I shot it into him with a water pistol.

48. *What is the end of everything?*
The letter G.

47. *When is a bicycle not a bicycle?*
When it turns into a driveway.

46. *Where do tough chickens come from?*
Hard-boiled eggs.

45. *How do you know when you have an elephant in bed with you?*
By the letter E embroidered on its pyjamas.

44. **WIFE:** *Stop the car quickly. I forgot to turn off the electric iron.*
HUSBAND: Don't worry, dear. I forgot to turn off the shower.

43. *Why did the chicken cross the road?*
To get away from Colonel Sanders.

42. *What kind of tea do they drink at Women's Lib meetings?*
Libber tea.

41. *What is the definition of debate?*
It's what lures de fish.

40. Did you hear about the Irishman who went bankrupt selling lucky charms?

39. *What would you call a highly educated and skilled plumber?*
A drain surgeon.

38. *How does a witch tell the time?*
With a witch watch.

37. *'What's your new sister's name?'*
'I don't know yet. We can't understand a word she says.'

36. *Why can't you bury people who live in houses opposite a graveyard?*
Because they are not dead yet.

35. 'Come on Johnny, tell me where you buried your dad in the sand. He's got the train tickets.'

34. *'Mummy, Mummy, my arms are tired.'*
'Be quiet and keep flying.'

33. My mother-in-law makes her own yoghourt. She buys a pint of milk and stares at it for a couple of minutes.

32. *'Doctor, Doctor, everyone thinks I'm a liar.'*
'I find that hard to believe.'

31. Did you hear about the Irish tramp who found the wooden box too hard to sleep on, so he stuffed it with straw?

30. FAT MAN: *You look as though you've been through a famine.*
THIN MAN: You look as though you've caused it.

29. 'Has your dog got a pedigree?'
    'Well, he has on his mother's side, but his father
        comes from a very good neighbourhood.'

28. *If the whole of Ireland should sink, what Irish city
        would remain afloat?*
    Cork.

27. *Why does the elephant wear ripple-soled shoes?*
    To give the ants a fifty-fifty chance.

26. FIRST DOG: *My name is Fido. What's yours?*
    SECOND DOG: I'm not sure, but I think it's Down Boy.

25. *What do you do with a sick wasp?*
    Take it to a waspital.

24. *If a lorry-load of eggs crashed into a milk lorry, what
        would you have?*
    A bloomin' great omelette.

23. *What is the definition of streaky bacon?*
    A pig running around with no clothes on.

22. *What is green, leafy and goes at around 120 mph?*
    A lettuce Elan.

21. *How do you spell contentment in four letters?*
    A. P. N. S. (Happiness)

20. POST OFFICE CLERK: *And what makes you think you
        should get a television licence for half price?*
    CUSTOMER: Because I've only got one eye.

19. LITTLE BILL: *Mummy, I feel as sick as a dog.*
    MUMMY: You lie down while I call the vet.

18. *What do you use to get back runaway rabbits?*
    Hare-restorer.

17. *What happens when 156 labourers fall off a mountainside?*
    You have a navvy-lanche.

16. *What did the cannibal have for lunch?*
    Baked beings on toast.

15. *What kind of car does Dracula drive?*
    A bloodmobile.

14. *How many peas in a pint?*
    Only one.

13. *When does a fire flare up?*
    When it is bellowed at.

12. *What did the hotel manager say to the elephant when he couldn't pay his bill?*
    'Pack your trunk and get out.'

11. Andy went shopping with his mother and the greengrocer gave him an apple.
    'What do you say, Andy?' said his mother.
    'Could you peel it please, Mister?' said Andy.

10. FIRST COMIC: *Why did you go into the cement business?*
    SECOND COMIC: Well, I've always been a good mixer.

9. *What happened when the man took his dog to the flea circus?*
He stole the show.

8. POLICEMAN: *You were driving at 90 mph, Miss.*
DRIVER: Isn't that wonderful? I only passed my test yesterday.

7. *'I had to have my dog put down.'*
'Was he mad?'
'Well, he wasn't too pleased about it.'

6. *'Doctor, my wife complains that I eat like a horse.'*
'Would you mind removing that nosebag? I can't hear a word you're saying.'

5. *What is the definition of lazy bones?*
A skeleton that doesn't like work.

4. WAITER: *Would you like to try some idiot soup, Sir?*
CUSTOMER: What's idiot soup?
WAITER: *Thick soup.*

3. *What letter is never found in the alphabet?*
The one you put in the post box.

2. *What do hangmen read?*
Noosepapers.

1. *What did one angel say to the other angel?*
'Halo . . . and . . .
Bye, Bye!'

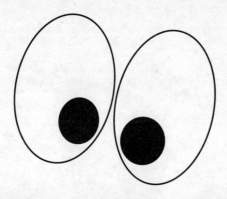

JOKES, JOKES, JOKES

a joke for every day of the year

GYLES BRANDRETH

illustrations by

SHELAGH McGEE

THIS BOOK IS DEDICATED TO THE MEMORY OF MY GOOD FRIENDS

Ida Hope
May Morning
Annie Seedball
Astrid de Stars
Ken John Peel
Luke Warm and
Eva Drawsoff*

(*They'd all be alive still if they hadn't read this book in typescript first. Unfortunately, reading it they all died laughing.)

January

1

What did Tarzan say when he saw the elephants coming?

'Here come the elephants!'

New Year's Day

2

What did Tarzan say when he saw the elephants coming wearing dark glasses?

Nothing. He didn't recognise them.

3

NEWS FLASH:
The marriage of two lighthouses keepers was said tonight to be on the rocks.

4

Did you hear about the beautiful young girl who kissed a Prince at a New Year's Eve party. He turned into a toad.

5

QUESTION OF THE WEEK:
What begins with T and ends with T and is full of T?
ANSWER OF THE WEEK:
A teapot!

6

Father: I've stopped our Willy from biting his nails.
Mother: *Oh, how did you do it dear?*
Father: I knocked all his teeth out.

Twelfth Night

7

Why do little birds in nest always agree?

Because they don't want to fall out.

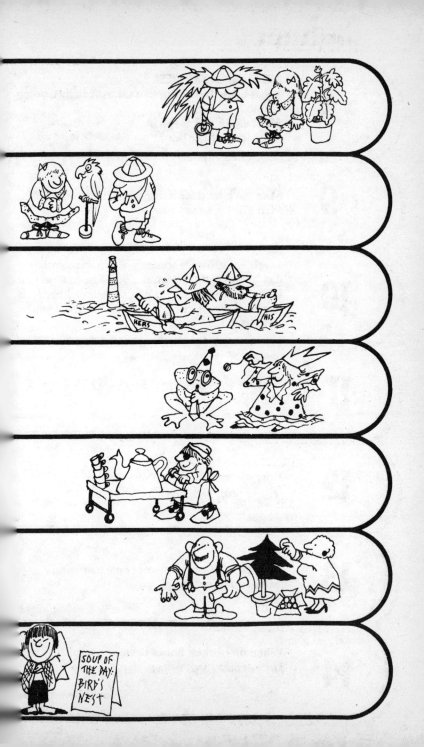

January

8

What is the last thing you take off before you go to bed?
ANSWER OF THE WEEK:
Your feet off the floor!

9

Max: Where does a frog hang his overcoat?
Mini: *In the croakroom!*

10

I walked into an ironmonger's shop the other day and asked the ironmonger if he had one inch nails. He said he had. I was so relieved because my back was itching so badly I needed someone to scratch it.

11

How do you start a pudding race?
SAGO!

12

How do you start a flea race?
One, two, flea . . . GO!

13

Why can the world never come to an end?
Because it's round!

14

When do broken bones become useful?
When they begin to knit!

National Beetroot D.

January

15

I often go for a tramp in the woods in January.
Fortunately for the tramp I don't often find him.

16

Jock: I'm sorry to hear your factory was burnt
down. What did you manufacture?
Dick: *Fire extinguishers.*

17

Jill: Do you know what you look like with your
eyes shut?
Jane: *No.*
Jill: Well, have a look in the mirror with your
eyes shut.

18

What's the difference between a gossip and an
umbrella?
You can shut up an umbrella!

19

SAYING OF THE WEEK:
My husband is so simple he even takes a saddle
and riding hat to bed with him in case of
nightmares.

20

I wouldn't say I was stupid, but when I went to
see a mindreader he did give me my money
back.

21

Business man: How is your typing speed
coming along, Miss Smith?
Miss Smith: *Oh, fine, thank you sir. Now I can
make twenty mistakes a minute.*

January

22
Bill: I hear the men are striking. What for?
Ben: *Shorter hours.*
Bill: Oh good. I always felt sixty minutes was too long for an hour.

23
Man: Good morning, Madam. I'm the piano tuner.
Mrs. Pye: *But I didn't send for you.*
Man: No, but your neighbours did.

24
NEWS FLASH: The Chairman of the Blotto Blotting Paper Company announced that he would not be retiring this year after all. He said he found his work totally absorbing.

25
POLICE NOTICE

Would the motorist who took the second turning off the M4 kindly put it back.

26
RIDDLE OF THE WEEK:

When is an unsharpened pencil like a bad joke?
When it has no point!

27
John: Why are feet like ancient tales?
Jack: *Because they are leg-ends.*

28
Oscar McTavish was a man after my own heart. He tried to stab me in the chest this morning.

January

29 What's vast and green and has a trunk?
An unripe elephant.

30 How do you make a Swiss roll?

The easiest way is to push him off the edge of an Alp!

31 Did you hear about the world's tiniest sailor? He was so small that he always slept on his watch.

SAVE OUR BEETROOTS

February

1
There were two men playing Scrabble. They played ten games and each man won nine games. **But that's impossible!**
No, it isn't. They were playing different people.

2
Why does an elephant have a trunk?
So that it has somewhere to hide when it sees a mouse.

3
Did you hear about the neurotic octopus? It was a crazy, mixed up squid!

4
The solicitor was reading out Albert's Will and reached the last sentence. 'And I always said I would mention my dear wife Doris in my Will,' read out the solicitor. 'So, hi there Doris!'

5
What does your watch say?
Tick, tock!

6
What does your watch say?
Tock, tick.
That's a bit odd, isn't it?
Yes, I'm afraid it's a bit backwards.

7
Does this train stop at Waterloo?
Well, there's going to be a right old smash-up if it doesn't.

National Mushroom Day

February

8

Why did the rhino lie down in the middle of the motorway?
To trip up the ants!

World Rhino Week

9

Why did the girl rhino paint her head yellow?
She wanted to find out if blondes had more fun!

10

How do you tell the difference between an elephant and a rhinoceros?
The elephant has a better memory.

11

How can you tell when there's a rhino in your sandwich?
When it's too heavy to lift!

12

Kojak: What's the difference between a rhino and a matterbaby?
Joe: *What's a matterbaby?*
Kojak: Nothing. What's the matter with you?

13

Bill: What's the difference between a lemon, a rhino and a tube of glue?
Ben: *You can squeeze a lemon, but you can't squeeze a rhino. But what about the glue?*
Bill: I thought that's where you'd get stuck.

14

What's the difference between a strawberry and a rhinoceros?
A strawberry is red.

Saint Valentine's Day

February

15

Shirley: I'm learning Ancient History.
Robert: *So am I. Why don't we go for a walk and talk over old times?*

16

RIDDLE OF THE WEEK:

Why is an empty room like a room full of married people?

Because there isn't a single person in it!

17

NEWS FLASH:

Owing to a strike at the meteorological office, there will be no weather tomorrow.

18

QUESTION OF THE WEEK:
What is a Metronome?

ANSWER OF THE YEAR:
A dwarf in the Paris Underground.

19

Businessman: Get out! I can't see you today.
Salesman: *Excellent, sir. I'm selling spectacles.*

20

John: Can you think of a bus that has crossed the Atlantic?
Jill: *Yes. Columbus.*

21

In Great Britain, where are Kings and Queens usually crowned?

On the head!

February

22

If a man smashed a grandfather clock, could he be accused of killing time?

Not if the clock struck first!

23

A man went to church to get married and found the vicar was planning to give him sixteen wives – four better, four worse, four richer, four poorer!

24

How do you makes notes out of stone?
I don't know. How do you make notes out of stone?
You just rearrange the letters!

25

What is the correct term for a water otter?
A kettle, of course!

26

What runs around all day with its sole-mate and then lies down all night with its tongue hanging out?
Your shoe, of course!

27

One toe turned to the other toe and whispered, 'Don't look now, but there's a heel following us.'

28

What is green, hairy and drinks from the wrong side of the glass?
A gooseberry trying to get rid of the hiccups!

World Hiccup Day

February

29

Alec: Some months have 31 days. Some months have 30 days. How many months have 28 days?

Rose: *February*.

Alec: No: all of them!

In Leap Years only

March

1

Dai the Bread is a Welsh baker.
Dye the Dress is a Welsh dry cleaner.
Die the Death is a Welsh undertaker.

Saint David's Day

2

'You know, at nights I snored so loudly I used to wake myself up.'
'What did you do about it?'
'Now I sleep in the next room I don't hear a thing.'

3

Count Dracula has an office in New York. It's on the thirteenth floor of the Vampire State Building.

4

Did you hear about the race between the cabbage, the tap and the tomato? The cabbage was ahead, the tap was running slowly and the tomato was trying to ketchup!

5

Have you heard about Will Knott? He's so lazy he signs his name: Won't

6

When there's a bank robbery, who is always the most talkative witness?
The teller, of course!

7

Teacher: Sheila, if you worked for seventeen hours and were paid £2.10 for every hour you worked, what would you get?
Sheila: *A new party dress.*

March

8

Today is the birthday of Gyles Brandreth, the much-loved author of this book and many other classics of contemporary literature. Birthday cards, bouquets and expensive presents should be sent to him care of his publishers.

9

SIGN IN A MAGISTRATES' COURT:

Thirty days hath September, April, June and the speeding offender!

10

Dai: How do people eat cheese in Wales?
Dylan: *Caerphilly.*

11

Customer: What's this leathery stuff, waiter?
Waiter: *Fillet of sole, sir.*
Customer: Take it away and see if you can't cut me a tender piece from the top of the boot.

12

Editor: Mac, did you get the story about the man who can sing bass and soprano at the same time?
Mac: *There's no story, sir. The man's got two heads.*

13

RIDDLE OF THE WEEK!

What pine has the longest and sharpest needles?
The porcupine!

14

A LITTLE BIT OF HISTORY:

At the time of the French Revolution many people went completely off their heads . . .

March

15
I met Sam Slopps today. You know he's working for the Water Board now. He's a bit of a drip really, but I asked him to drop by one day.

16
Voice on the phone: Is that the zoo keeper?
Zoo Keeper: *It is.*
Voice: Oh good. My son's having a birthday party tomorrow and I wondered if you had any ideas of what I could do?

17
RIDDLE FOR SAINT PATRICK'S DAY:
Why is it so hard to believe in the Blarney Stone?
Because there are a lot of sham rocks in Ireland.
Saint Patrick's Day

18
My grandmother is incredible. She's ninety-two and she hasn't got a grey hair on her head. She's totally bald.

19
Little Rodney: Oh, Mummy, I feel as sick as a dog.
Mummy: *Don't worry, dear. I'll call the vet.*

20
Customer: Waiter! Call the manager. – I can't eat this stew!
Waiter: *It's no use, sir. The manager won't eat it either.*

21
QUESTION OF THE MOMENT:
How do you cut through the waves?

ANSWER OF THE MOMENT:
With a sea-saw!

March

22

Why will you never starve in the desert?
Because of the sand which is there!

National Daffodil Week

23

What's enormous, white, fluffy and hangs from the rafters of the cake shop just outside London Zoo?
A meringue-outang!

24

Why does the baby elephant walk softly?
Because it's a baby still and can't walk, hardly!

25

One of the greatest of all works of literature is the novel **Great Eggspectations**. It was written by Charles Chickens.

26

What lives in the winter, dies in the summer and grows with its roots upwards?
What?
An icicle!

27

Why did the pussy cat join the St. John's Ambulance Brigade?
Because it wanted to be a first aid kit!

28

What did the baby hedgehog say when it backed into a cactus?
'Is that you, mother?'

March

29

What goes da-da-da-croak, dot-dot-croak, da-dot-da-croak?
A Morse toad!

30

Why do elephants paint themselves red?
Why?
So that they can hide in cherry trees.
Have you ever seen an elephant in a cherry tree?
No, which proves how effective it is.

31

'I believe in getting to the bottom of things,' said the angry father as he spanked his naughty son.

April

1

There is no joke for today because today you should be too busy fooling other people to have time to laugh at one of our jokes!

April Fool's Day

2

Why isn't a nose twelve inches long?
Because then it would be a foot!

3

Jock: Dad, that dentist wasn't painless like he said he was.
Dad: *Why? Did he hurt you?*
Jock: No, but he screamed when I bit his finger, just like any other dentist.

4

NEWS FLASH:
The new plan to wrap all meat pies in tin has just been foiled.

5

What do you call high-rise flats for pigs?
Styscrapers!

6

Why is it dangerous to leave a clock at the top of the stairs?
Because it might run down!

7

Which is the oldest tree?
The elder!

International Ostrich Day

April

8

To avoid that run down feeling, look both ways before crossing.

9

Explorer: Why are you looking at me like that?
Cannibal: *Because I'm the food inspector.*

10

NEWS FLASH:
A man jumped into a river in Paris this morning in an attempt to kill himself. He was said to be in Seine.

11

What can't you name without breaking it?
Silence.

12

Did you hear what the metal-noticeboard said this morning? 'You can't pin anything on me.'

13

If ghosts go for a short spring holiday at the seaside in April, where do they usually stay?
At ghost houses!

14

When do your teeth resemble your tongue?
When they start to chatter!

April

15

Bill: What's the difference between a tuna fish and a grand piano?
Ben: *I don't know.*
Bill: You can't tune a fish!

16

Waiter: How did you find the pork chop, sir?
Diner: *By accident – I moved the chip and there it was!*

17

NEWS FLASH:
A dry cleaner was excused jury service yesterday because he said his business was pressing.

18

What is green, leafy and travels at over 100 m.p.h.?
A lettuce elan!

19

What is the difference between an elephant and a flea?
An elephant can have fleas, but a flea can't have elephants.

20

Fanny: How do you make gold soup?
Johnny: *You have to start with fourteen carrots.*

21

HORRID RIDDLE OF THE WEEK:

Why shouldn't a pig get sick?
Because he'll have to be killed before he can be cured.

April

22

Willy: With what two animals do you always go to bed?
Billy: *Two calves!*

23

Julian: What are you taking for your cold?
Janet: *What will you give me?*

24

Patient: I feel funny, doctor. What should I do?
Doctor: *Become a comedian!*

Saint George's Day

25

NEWS FLASH: A man walked through the centre of Birmingham today wearing only a newspaper. He told police that he always liked to dress with *The Times*.

26

What two letters spell jealousy?
NV

27

Why couldn't the orange run down hill?
Because it had run out of juice!

28

What is yours but used by others more than it is used by yourself?
Your name!

April

29 'I have a pressing engagement,' said the man as he took his trousers to the dry cleaners.

30 What did the toothpaste say to the toothbrush?

'Give us a squeeze and I'll meet you outside the Tube.'

May

1
The only thing I know about Margaret of Anjou is that she was incredibly fat. I know that because I once read in a history book, 'Margaret of Anjou was King Henry's stoutest supporter.'

2
Doctor: Are you still taking the cough mixture I gave you?
Patient: *No. I tasted it once and decided I'd rather have the cough.*

3
Did you hear about the unhappy compass? It complained that it was always going round in circles.

4
What do you get when you drop a grand piano down a mine shaft?
You get A Flat Minor!

5
And what do you get when you drop a grand piano into an army barracks?
You get A Flat Major!

6
NEWS FLASH: A strawberry was reported this afternoon to be in a bit of a jam.

7
What can you give away and still keep?
A cold!

ASHoo!

May

8

What jumps out of the North Sea shouting, 'Knickers! Knickers!'
Crude oil!

9

And what jumps out of the North Sea shouting, 'Underwear! Underwear!'
Refined oil!

10

Jill: Look at that broken down old shack. I wonder what keeps it together?
Jack: *The woodworms are holding hands.*

11

Why should fish be better educated than frogs?
Because fish live in schools!

12

NEWS FLASH: Ten tons of human hair to be made into wigs was stolen from New York today. Police are now combing the area.

13

How long will an eight-day clock run without winding?
It won't run at all without winding.

14

'Tough luck,' said the egg in the monastery. 'It's out of the frying-pan into the Friar.'

National Poppycock Day

May

15 Have you ever thought how parents spend the first part of a child's life encouraging him to walk and talk, and the rest of his childhood telling him to sit down and be quiet.

16 **NEWS FLASH:** Under the Government's latest pay policy, barbers are no longer to get fringe benefits.

17 Why is the American hot dog the noblest of all animals?
Because it feeds the hand that bites it!

18 Why is a promise like an egg?
Because both are so easily broken!

19 What is yellow and goes 'Clunch Clunch'?
A Chinaman eating potato crisps.

20 **Joe:** Did you hear what one herring said to the other herring?
Jim: 'I am my brother's kipper!'

21 What is the difference between a book and a bore?
You can shut up a book!

May

22

Ned: What do you do with a green banana?
Fred: *Teach it something.*

23

Man: Do you think pineapples are happy?
Other man: *Well, I've never heard one complain.*

24

NEWS FLASH: Yesterday a thousand men walked out of a steel mill while it was still in operation. The chief Shop Steward said they had decided to strike while the iron was hot.

25

What do you give sick rabbits?
Hare tonic!

26

What goes uphill and downhill, but always stays in the same place?
The road!

27

Doctor: Don't you know my hours are from 9 until 12?
Patient: *Yes, but the mad dog that bit me didn't.*

28

QUESTION OF THE WEEK:
What vegetable needs a plumber?

ANSWER OF THE WEEK:
The leek!

FRUIT STALL

May

29

John: If you had only one match and you went into a room where there was a candle, a gas lamp and a stove, what would you light first?
Jill: *The candle.*
John: No, the match!

30

'This is the end!' cried the little boy as his braces broke and his trousers fell down.

31

Who was Ivanhoe?
A Russian gardener!

June

1

Dentist: Please stop screaming. I haven't even touched your tooth yet.
Patient: *I know, but you're treading on my foot.*

2

NEWS FLASH: A dumpling was reported this morning as being in a bit of a stew.

3

QUESTION OF THE MONTH:
How many balls of string would it take to reach from the earth to the moon?
ANSWER OF THE MONTH:
Only one if it was long enough.

4

Bill: Why is it dangerous to play cards in the jungle?
Ben: *Because of all the cheetahs!*

5

What falls often in winter but never gets hurt?
Snow!

6

Have you heard about the new doll surgeon?
You just wind it up and it operates on batteries!

7

What does a lamb become after it is one year old?
Two years old.

June

8 How would an elephant smell without his trunk?
He'd still smell.

9 Why are elephants flat-footed?
Because they're always jumping up and down with pleasure at hearing all those dreadful elephant jokes.

10 How can you get five elephants into a mini?
You can't. You could probably get two in the front and two in the back, but the fifth elephant would definitely have to walk.

11 What did the grape say when the elephant trod on it?
Nothing. It just let out a little whine.

12 How does one elephant get down from a tree?
It climbs onto a leaf and waits till autumn.

13 How does another elephant get down from a tree?
It doesn't. It gets down from a duck.

14 How can you tell if there's an elephant in the refrigerator?
By the footprints in the butter.

June

15

Bill: What's the best thing to put in a pie?
Ben: *Your teeth!*

16

What happens when you cross a giant elk with a pound of cocoa powder?
You get a chocolate moose!

17

Doris: Edna, I think your husband dresses nattily.
Edna (alarmed): *Natalie who?*

18

RIDDLE OF THE WEEK:

What words can be pronounced quicker and shorter by adding another syllable to them?
QUICK and SHORT.

19

Sam: Where does a ghost-train stop?
Sally: *At a manifestation!*

20

Willy: My dad makes faces all day.
Julia: *Really? Why?*
Willy: He works in a clock factory.

21

QUESTION OF THE DAY:
What do you call pigs that like each other?

ANSWER OF THE MINUTE:
Pen friends!

June

22

Will : Why can only very small gnomes and fairies sit underneath toadstools?
Jill : *Because there is not mushroom!*

23

Bob : Who always goes to sleep with his shoes on?
Tom : *I don't know. Who?*.
Bob : A horse!

24

Why did the elephant leave the circus?
He got tired of working for peanuts!

25

QUESTION OF THE WEEK:
Where do shellfish raise money on their valuables?
ANSWER OF THE MOMENT:
In a prawn-shop.

26

NEWS FLASH: The President of the International Periscope Manufacturers Association said today that business was looking up.

27

Did you hear what happened to the two burglars who stole a calendar? They each got six months

28

What did one candle say to the other candle?
'You're getting on my wick.'

June

29

Why do elephants wear slippers?

So that they can sneak up on mice without being heard.

30

What did the idiot call his pet leopard?

Spot.

July

1

Mick: Miss, I eaten seven eggs for breakfast.
Miss: *Ate, Mick ate.*
Mick: It might have been eight, Miss, but I
      know I eaten an awful lot.

2

THOUGHT OF THE WEEK:
A graveyard is never deserted. You are always
sure to find some body there.

3

If two's company and three's a crowd, what are
four and five?
NINE!

4

Master of Disguise: You know, this isn't my
      own moustache I'm wearing. My real one's
      in my pocket.

5

Collector: But this can't be George
      Washington's skull. It's far too small.
Dealer: *Oh, but I forgot to tell you. It was his
      skull when he was a little boy.*

6

What do you do with a wombat?
Play wom, of course!

7

My mother always believed in germ free food.
She used to put arsenic in my sandwiches to
make sure she killed them.

July

8

SIGN OF THE TIMES

CROSS ROAD
(Better Humour It!)

9

Sam: I had a fall last night that kept me
      unconscious for nearly nine hours.
Jim: *Oh dear, where did you fall?*
Sam: I fell asleep.

10

What does Her Majesty the Queen do when she
burps?
She issues a Royal Pardon!

11

Did you hear what that carpet said to the floor
today? 'Don't move. I've got you covered.'

12

Why are a pastry cook's hands like a July
garden?
Both are in flower!

13

Teacher: As you know, all the animals that
       came to Noah's ark came in pairs.
Tommy: *That's not true. The two worms came in
       apples.*

14

What did the earth say when it rained?
If this keeps up my name will be mud!

July

15

Jane: Did you ever hear the joke about the smashed packet of biscuits?
John: *No.*
Jane: Well, its crumby!

16

QUESTION OF THE DAY:
Where do baby beans come from?

ANSWER OF THE HOUR:
They are brought by the stalk!

17

Ladies and gentlemen, meet Anna Stetic! This girl's a real knock-out!

18

Notice to be placed in all gardens in July:
'Anyone is welcome to come and borrow our lawn mower, as long as he doesn't take it out of our garden.'

19

Phil: You know I always get up when the first ray of sunlight hits my window.
Jill: *Isn't that rather early?*
Phil: No. My room faces West.

20

What is very beautiful, sits on flowers and is highly dangerous?
A man-eating butterfly!

21

Who are the world's three unluckiest ladies?
Miss Chance
Miss Fortune
Miss Hap

ON-
THE
SPOT
HIRE

July

22 How do you think Jack Frost gets to work?
By icicle, I suppose.

23 Dad: How do you like going to school, Jimmy?
Jimmy: I like going to school, Dad. And I like coming home from school. It's the time in between I hate.

24 How did the man-eating tiger feel after he had eaten a whole pillow?
Down in the mouth!

25 I've always believed in love at first sight – ever since I looked into a mirror.

National Be Kind to Tadpoles Day

26 Secretary: The Invisible Man is waiting for you, Sir Eric.
Sir Eric: *Tell him I can't see him.*

27 Teacher (answering telephone): You say Johnny Johnson has a bad cold and can't come to school today. To whom am I speaking?
Voice: *Oh, this is my father.*

28 Did you hear about the human cannonball at the Ringling Brothers Circus? He got fired.

July

29

There was this man working in a butcher's shop who was six feet tall and wore size 10 shoes. What did he weigh?
I don't know.
Meat!

30

How many sides has a circle?
A circle doesn't have sides.
Yes, it does. The inside and the outside!

31

How do you communicate with fish?
You just drop them a line!

August

1

Why did the man with only one hand cross the road?

To get to the second-hand shop!

2

What's in the middle of Paris, five hundred metres tall and always wet?

The Eiffel Shower!

3

There's only one flower that grows on your face: Tulips!

Nonsense! I've got roses in my cheeks.

4

There are three inventions that have helped Man get up in the world; do you know what they are?

The lift, the escalator and the alarm clock!

5

Teacher: Nathaniel, what is the Order of the Bath?
Nathaniel: *Dad, Mum, my sister Clare, then me.*

6

There's only one way to get into a locked cemetery at night. You use a skeleton key.

7

Lucy: Mummy, my teacher punished me for something I didn't do.
Mummy: *What was that, dear?*
Lucy: My homework!

August

8

Tall fat man in the cinema to little boy
     sitting behind him: Can you see, sonny?
Little boy: No.
Man: Don't worry. Just laugh when I do.

9

Where does it cost £20 a head to eat?
In a Cannibal Café.

10

When asked to make a contribution to the local
orphanage, my friend Sila O'Twit sent two
orphans.

11

I have four legs, but only one foot. What am I?
A bed.

12

What goes Ha Ha Ha Bonk?
A man laughing his head off!

13

Tim: What did the love-sick moon-boy say to
    the love-sick moon-girl?
Tom: *Oh, how romantic! There's a beautiful full-
    earth out tonight!*

14

What is hot, greasy and makes you unhappy?
A chip on the shoulder.

August

15 Why do you say Amen in church instead of Awomen?
Same reason as you sing Hymns instead of Hers.

16 Who was the cowboy who had twelve guns and terrorised the ocean bed?
Billy the Squid!

17 You know that owls never feel romantic when it's been raining. That's when they sit on the branches of the trees where they live and call out, 'Too wet to woo! To wet to woo!'

18 What wears shoes, but has no feet?
The pavement!

International Have-a-Plate-of-Chips-Today Day

19 Nervous passenger: Do these planes often crash?
Air hostess: *Only once.*

20 Did you hear about Romeo and Juliet. They met in a revolving door – and they've been going round together ever since.

21 How could you go without sleep for seven whole nights and still not be tired?
By sleeping through the days.

August

22

Ron: Do insects have brains?
Edna: Of course, insects have brains. How else do you think they'd work out where we were going to have our picnic.

23

THOUGHT OF THE MONTH:

The cheapest time to ring your friends is . . . when they're out!

24

If I put a dozen ducks into this old wooden box what will I have?
A box of quackers!

25

What do you get when you cross a sheep with a thunderstorm?
A wet blanket!

26

How did the philosopher manage to get the elephant to cross the English Channel without using a boat or a plane?
He just thought it over!

27

American boy: Do you want something swell?
English boy: *Yes please!*
American boy: Okay, bend down and I'll hit you on the head with this milk bottle.

28

Have you heard about the latest development in gardening? People are getting cows to cut the grass. They call them Lawn Moo-ers!

August

29

Why do wizards and witches always drink tea?

Because sorcerers need cuppas!

30

Jack: I weighed only three pounds when I was born.

Jill: *Did you live?*

Jack: Did I live! You should see me now!

31

There were three men in a boat with four cigarettes but no matches. You'll never believe what they did. They threw out one cigarette and made the boat a cigarette lighter!

September

1

Oh, Doris, I'm so sorry to hear your uncle died in a barrel of varnish. What a way to go!
'He had a beautiful finish.'

Celebrate Saint Giles' Day

2

What do you do with sick budgies?
¡pǝʇǝǝʍʇ ɯǝɥʇ ǝʌɐH

3

Interviewer: Can you play any musical instruments?
Rock star: *Yeah. I'm very good on the barrel organ.*

4

Ron: Mum, all the boys at school called me a girl!
Mum: *What did you do, dear?*
Ron: Hit them with my handbag!

5

Jack: Is your electric toaster a pop-up model?
Jill: *No, it's a Red Indian model.*
Jack: What's that?
Jill: *The toaster that sends up smoke signals.*

6

Billy: Do you mean to tell me you fell over fifty feet and didn't get hurt.
Sally: *Yes. I was just trying to get to the back of the bus.*

7

What do you call the man who owns all the cows in Arabia?
¡ɥʞᴉǝɥs ʞlᴉɯ ǝɥ⊥

September

8

How can you recognise a dogwood tree?

ANSWER OF THE YEAR:
By its bark!

9

What do cats read every morning?
Mewspapers.
And gnus?
Gnuspapers!

10

I learnt to swim at a very early age. My parents used to take me out to the middle of a large lake and drop me over the edge of the boat so that I had to swim to the shore all on my own. I loved the swim. It was getting out of the sack that was difficult.

11

When you look round on a very cold day, what do you see on every hand?
A glove!

12

What did the baby chicks say when they saw their mother lay an orange?
'Look what Marmalade!'

13

What has six feet and sings?
A trio!

14

THINGS YOU NEVER SAW:

A shoe box!
A salad bowl!
A square dance!

September

15

Why is it dangerous to tell a secret down on a farm?

Because the potatoes have eyes, the corn has ears and the beans talk!

16

Why can't two elephants go into the sea at the same time?

Because between them they have only got one pair of trunks!

17

GREAT SAYINGS OF OUR TIME:
'I love kids. I used to go to school with them.'

18

Why is a lord like a book?
Because they both have a title!

National Hop Up & Down Day

19

Young Agricultural Student: Your methods of cultivation are very old-fashioned. For example, I'd be very surprised if you got more than six pounds of apples from that tree.
Old Farmer: *So would I. It's a cherry tree.*

20

What do misers do during a cold September?
Sit round a candle!

21

In prehistoric times, what did they call ship disasters at sea?
Tyrannosaurus Wrecks!

September

22

Scout leader: You're facing North. On your left is the East. On your right is the North. What's at your back?
Scout: *My rucksack!*

23

In Wales they call an underwater swimmer a Dai Ver and a by-pass a Dai Version!

24

Did you hear about the poor man who went to see the psychiatrist because he spent all the time curled up underneath his bed? He thought he was a little potty.

25

Victorian schoolmaster: Switzerland is as big as Siam. Now, Basil, are you paying attention. How big is Switzerland?
Basil: *As big as you are, Sir.*

26

'Where's your pencil, Roy?' *'I ain't got none.'* 'How many times do I have to tell you? It's I haven't got one. You haven't got one. We haven't got one. They haven't got one.' *'Yes, well, where are all the pencils then if nobody ain't got none?'*

27

What's old and grey and travels at 100 m.p.h.?
An E-type Grannie.

28

The Punk Rock group threw a stick of dynamite into the middle of the audience. That really brought the house down.

September

29   The surgeon cleared his throat – by removing his tonsils, adenoids, tongue, teeth and gums.

30   What begins with P, ends with E and contains thousands of letters?
The Post Office!

PABCDEFGHIJK

October

1

Soldiers mark time with their feet. What does the same thing with its hands?
A clock!

October is International Gooseberry Month

2

My grandfather used to think he was a budgerigar. But he went to a marvellous psychiatrist who really helped him and recently we haven't heard a peep out of him.

3

NEWS FLASH:
Earlier today the chairmen of two rival electric fire manufacturers were heard having a heated argument.

4

What is cold, green and red and talks back when you lick it?
An ice polly!

5

POLICE NOTICE
Man wanted for burglary. Apply within.

6

Doctor: And what's that old miser complaining about now?
Nurse: He says he got better long before that medicine you gave him was all used up.

7

QUESTION OF THE WEEK:
What would be the best thing to do if you decided you were mad?
ANSWER OF THE WEEK:
Change your mind!

October

8

What's the hardest part of learning to ride a bike?
The pavement!

9

How do you make anti-freeze?
Stick her in the refrigerator!

10

Lord Ptolemy Ffitch-Fitzwilliams was born with a silver spoon in his mouth. Once it was taken out, he was quite all right.

11

If a church caught fire, what would be sure to burn even if the fire brigade arrived in time?
The organ – because the hose couldn't play on it!

12

If you like grave humour, you might enjoy the story about the two body-snatchers. On second thoughts, perhaps I won't tell it. You might get carried away.

13

Policeman: Can I help you, Sir?
Old man: *Yes, officer. I've lost a toffee.*
Policeman: Oh, I thought it was something important.
Old Man: *It is. My teeth are in it.*

14

HORRID RIDDLE OF THE WEEK:

What has four legs and flies?
A dead horse!

October

15

What's French, very wobbly, tall and tasty?
The Trifle Tower!

International Jelly Week

16

Max: I think your school must be haunted.
Jim: *Why do you think that?*
Max: Well, your headmaster is always talking about the school spirit.

17

What should you call a bald koala?
Fred Bare!

18

Sensible people always carry olive oil around with them – just in case they bump into an olive that happens to need oiling.

19

When is an opera singer not an opera singer?
When he's a little hoarse!

20

Willy: Hey, Mum, the old clothes man is at the door.
Mum: *Say no, Willy. We've already got plenty of old clothes of our own.*

21

Fatty: I'm disgusted.
Friend: *Why?*
Fatty: I stepped onto the Speak-Your-Weight Weighing Machine today and it said 'One person at a time please.'

October

22

Jenny: Aren't you rather hot doing all that painting dressed up like that?
Ginny: *Well, it says here on the paint pot to be sure to put on at least two coats!*

23

The City gentleman was served with Minestrone inside his hat.
Why?
Because he asked for a bowler soup.

24

Baby girl showing her friend the scales in the bathroom: 'All I know is that you stand on it and it makes you furious.'

25

My father was a very religious man, you know. He wouldn't work if there was a Sunday in the week.

26

Why do cows like lying on sunny beaches?
Because they enjoy tanning their hides.

27

Tax Inspector: As a good citizen you should pay your taxes with a smile.
Business man: *That's what I want to do, but you keep asking for money!*

28

Don't you think that new overcoat of yours is a bit loud?
It'll be all right when I put on a muffler.

October

29

'I went to the theatre last night, but I left after the first Act.'
'*Why?*'
'I couldn't wait that long. It said on the programme: Act Two – Five Years Later.'

30

What is the best way to avoid falling hair?
Jump out of the way!

31

What do Eskimoes call the big, formal dances they have at Christmas?
Snowballs!

Hallowe'en

November

1
When is a man-eating tiger most likely to enter a house?
I don't know. When?
When the door's open!

2
When do Red Indians have to wear buckets over their heads?
When they want to become pale faces!

3
How do frogs and rabbits make beer?
I don't know, but I'm sure they start with some hops.

4
Doctor: What's the matter then?
Patient: *I'm so worried. I keep thinking I'm a pair of curtains.*
Doctor: Don't worry and pull yourself together!

5
Guy Fawkes: Can you spell Blind Pig?
Mrs Fawkes: *B-L-I-N-D P-I-G.*
Guy Fawkes: Wrong. It's B-L-N-D P-G. With two I's he wouldn't be blind.'

6
How did the Mexican detective know that Juan Donmingez had been killed with a Golf Gun?
Because it had definitely made a hole in Juan!

7
To what regiment in the army do baby soldiers always belong?
The Infantry!

November

8

Bill: Ouch! That water's just burned my hand.
Ben: *Well, silly, you should have felt it before putting your hand in.*

9

What did the Sugar Plum Fairy call her house?
Gnome Sweet Gnome!

10

Mrs. McTavish's boy Rory went off to join the army. After six months he wrote to her to say he'd grown another foot. So, sensible woman, she knitted him another sock.

11

You know what's the best kind of paper to use when you're making a kite?
No. What?
Flypaper!

12

What is brown, shiny and flies the Atlantic at 1,400 m.p.h.?
The Anglo-French Conker!

13

Did you hear about the little boy who went to the street corner to watch the traffic jam? A lorry came along and gave him a jar.

14

Giles: I'm going to buy a farm two hundred miles long and half-an-inch wide.
Jolyon: *What on earth are you going to grow?*
Giles: Spaghetti!

BEST
TRAFFIC
CONSERVE

November

15

What is French for 'I am an Australian'?
I don't know. What?
'Moi Aussi'!

16

Have you heard about the little girl who was afraid she was dying? She went and sat in the living room and felt a lot better.

17

Wee Willy in the First Form: Oh, Miss Hoskins, I like you so much. You're a lovely teacher. I'm just so sorry you're not bright enough to teach us next year when we're in the Second Form.

18

In 1939 hundreds of English families moved into the city because they heard the country was at war!

19

What did one rock pool say to the other rock pool?
'Show us your mussels!'

20

I've only just realised why Robin Hood only ever robbed the rich. He knew the poor didn't have anything.

21

Prince Charming: 'You know, I've believed in reincarnation ever since I was a young frog.'

November

22
Minnie: My Granny can play the piano by ear.
Mickey: *That's nothing. My Grandad fiddles with his whiskers.*

23
Why do the African elephants have big ears?
Because Noddy refused to pay the ransom!

24
I slept very badly last night, you know.
'Really. Why?'
Well, I plugged my electric blanket into the toaster by mistake and I spent the whole night popping out of bed.

25
QUESTION OF THE MONTH:
If the plug doesn't fit, do you socket?

26
'I'm afraid I've just run over your cat. I'm so sorry. Can I replace it?'
'That's very good of you, but do you think you'll be able to catch mice?'

27
Repair Man: I've come to repair your door bell.
Mrs. Jones: *But you should have come yesterday.*
Repair Man: I did. I rang the bell five times and got no answer.

28
Why don't elephants ride bicycles?
Because their thumbs can't work the bell.

November

29

Holifernes: Mummy, I'm really glad you called me Holifernes.
Mummy: *Why dear?*
Holifernes: Because that's what they call me at school.

30

When is the best time to buy budgies?
When they're going cheep!

Saint Andrew's Day

December

1

Joe: Did you hear the joke about the rope?
Jack: *No.*
Joe: Then let's skip it.

2

SIGN OUTSIDE A LADIES' HAIRDRESSERS:

WE CURL UP AND DYE FOR YOU!

3

If you have an umpire in tennis and cricket and a referee in football and rugger, what do you have in bowls?
Goldfish!

4

NEWS FLASH: Late last night a huge hole was cut in the wooden fence surrounding Saint Vitus's Nudist Camp near Broadstairs. People are looking into it.

5

What ship has no captain but two mates?
Courtship.

6

Mr and Mrs Smith had just adopted a little baby girl who came to them from France. At the same time they started taking French lessons so that they'd know what the baby was saying as soon as it began to talk.

7

What is bright red and very stupid?
A blood clot!

December

8 Once upon a time there was a little boy called Merlin. He was an amazing magician. He went around a corner and turned into a sweetshop!

9 There's a new kind of soap on the market. It's ten foot high and four foot wide. Instead of lifting it up to wash with. You sit on it and slide up and down.

10 What do you call an egg that loves April Fools?
A practical yolker!

11 Why is it always cold at football matches?
Because of all the fans that are there!

12 Lady Godiva was so shy, she had to go into a dark room even to change her mind.

13 **Adam:** And I shall call that creature a hippopotamus.
Eve: *But why, dear?*
Adam: Because it looks like a hippopotamus, stupid!

14 There's only one way to put yourself through a keyhole. Write 'yourself' on a tiny piece of paper and pass it through the keyhole!

December

15

What's the cheapest way to hire a car?
Put bricks under the wheels!

National Giggler's Week

16

Why did the girl put her bed in the fireplace?
Because she wanted to sleep like a log.

17

Tim: (answering telephone): Hello.
Voice: *Hello. Is Boo there?*
Tim: Boo who?
Voice: *Don't cry little boy. I must have got the wrong number.*

18

What goes in dry, comes out wet and pleases people?
A tea bag!

19

The question every angler is asking himself this December: Does fishing result in net profits?

20

What should you do if you split your sides laughing?
I don't know. What?
Run until you get a stitch in them!

21

Where should two motorists have a swordfight?
On a duel carriage way, of course!

December

22 SIGN IN A GOLF CLUB:

BACK SOON. GONE TO TEE.

23 **NEWS FLASH:** Yesterday a lady dropped her handbag over the edge of the railway platform. The porters refused to retrieve the handbag as they considered it beneath their station.

24 What do you call a tug of war on 24 December?
Christmas 'Eave!

25 Who is Santa Claus' wife?
Mary Christmas!

Christmas Day

26 Why does an ill-mannered Communist called Alfred always stay indoors during wet weather?
Because Rude Alf, the Red, knows Rain, Dear!

Boxing Day

27 **Jill:** There are several things I can always count on.
Jack: *What are they?*
Jill: My fingers.

28 What part of London is in France?
The letter N!

December

29 Why are they not going to grow bananas any longer?

Because they're long enough already!

30 How can you tell when there's an elephant under your bed?

When your nose hits the ceiling.

31 What comes at the end of every year?

The letter R!

New Year's Eve